New Kid On The Block

The Art of Starting Over

New Kid On The Block

Block

The Art of Starting Over

Yolanda D. Mercer

New Kid On The Block
The Art of Starting Over
Yolanda D. Mercer

Dedicated to my mother and her mother

Brenda Mercer and Lena Mercer

I am because of you

4

New Kid On The Block

The Art of Starting Over

Migration Is Expensive…….…..……….…..……11
The Remix – Surrendering In Uncertainty…....…27
Rookie of the Year…….……….………………...44
Discomfort of Destiny……………….…………54
The Pivot Is Not A Punishment………….……..65
New Normal……………………….………….84
The New Kids………………………………….99
Turn The Page…………………………………119
The Exit Plan………………………...………139
About the Author……………………………160

Introduction

Introduction

Mastering the art of starting over is no easy task. Shifting your mind from the intricate details that you've become so accustomed to in life can be a daunting experience. When what you know is unrecognizable, when what you understand is unreachable, and when what you love is unapproachable; life as you know it can feel unbearable.

Can you imagine being ripped from the comfortable world that once wrapped around you so tightly with familiarity and ease? Can you picture being dropped smack dab in the middle of a foreign space that wherever you turned you just couldn't find home? I can because I experienced it first-hand. I'll tell you a little bit more about that in the New Normal chapter. No place is common. No road leads to havens. There is no yellow brick pathway that guides your steps to an epiphany of enlightenment. This time, Dorothy, we're definitely not in Kansas anymore and we won't be going back.

The path to your destiny is the path of the unknown. It's a path that pulls on the heartstrings of your courage and shoestrings of your steps. If feet could talk they'd tell a story of fear and apprehension that desired to stop at every round.

They'd tell a story of doubt and discouragement that prayed to reverse every pivot along the way. What is starting over anyway? What does that actually mean? To begin to do something again, sometimes in a different way. Making a new beginning. To begin to happen again. These words and phrases suggest that the direction is in motion as opposed to being stuck. These words: begin, new beginning are terms of movement. You cannot start over without movement. You cannot start over without motion. In order to start you can no longer be stuck.

Becoming unstuck requires becoming unhinged; unhinged from the same cycle, unhinged from the same trajectory of life. It's amazing how at the snap of a finger your life can be hit with swift transition. Who would have thought that the only way to get ahead is to get unstuck. Not only does starting over takes courage, but starting over takes vision. You have to see it before you see it. You have to envision yourself moving forward before you visit yourself moving fearlessly. Yes I said visit yourself.

When you visit yourself, you self-reflect on the moves you've made. You gain introspection of the decisions you've developed. You visit the thought of starting fresh over and over in your mind. It's so real you feel it. It's so close you can taste it.

Starting over takes courage. It takes courage because you have to know why you're starting over. There's no easy way to start over and knowing why is the first step. Whether you are starting over after a relationship, starting over after the end of a career, or starting over after an unexpected move; to wrestle in the weight of the transition is our only option. It's only when you reach that point, when the tears have ceased and the rapid pace of thoughts swiftly chase your dreams and the whatifs are invited to dinner; that you realize you're at the starting point yet again.

Can I tell you a secret? We have a choice. Your steps are ordered, but your steps are your choices. Even when it seems like there's literally no way to stabilize this crazy whirlwind of change, we must believe that there is always a choice. We have the choice to freely rewrite the script of our mind. We have the choice to joyfully redevelop the blueprint of our plans.

Most of us are actually pretty petrified of failure. Not that it's ever been second nature to desire to embrace our faults with joy, but in a day and time where fairytales are created with spins, sarcasm, and scrutiny; no one signs up to say I failed. Even if you're starting over because you failed, chances are it feels so devastating that it continually grips a hold in the breakable cycle of thoughts that grip

9

your mind. Again, starting over is a choice. There are no overarching forces dictating your need to obsess over your seemingly lack of progression without the added weight of surprise now that it's being experienced. Let's be honest, endings don't feel good when you encounter them and starting over because of them is even worse. It's truly as if your heart is synced to the harmony of a completely different song that you weren't prepared to sing. There's nothing that can soften the blow of starting over when you thought that you were done.

Even though it does not always feel good, starting over can be an incredible opportunity to reclaim the present realization that all we truly have is right now. When you encounter an ending, only you can decide when to transition that ending into a new beginning. When you first allow yourself to acknowledge that seasons do exist, you'll have an easier time stepping into your next and believing that greater is coming. What's amazing about the future is, the only thing that's predictable is the unpredictable. This ripe experience proves the undeniable power of God's sovereign grace to abound in every season. So let's get started!

Migration Is Expensive

Migration Is Expensive

Have you ever experienced such a transition in your life that swept you off your feet? I'm talking about a change that cascaded discomfort down your spine, built a catalyst of adjustments, and molded the trajectory of your life. When you least expect it, God will hand deliver the biggest package of your life strategically marked, handle with care. Managing such a transition requires the most massive pair of big girl panties wrapped in courage, boldness, and a level of fearlessness that stands in the face of the most tumultuous change. This kind of transition is called starting over.

It takes courage to start over. It takes courage to be an immigrant. True immigration is leaving your familiar environment in order to gain progress in a new territory. True immigration is migrating uncertainly to a fresh start yet frightening decision. Immigrants require bravery because what you just left places a mandate on what you have to find. Immigrants require boldness because immediately upon arrival you configure layouts, you calculate finances, you surveillance environments, you inspect surroundings, you study culture, you discover regulations. Migration is expensive. It costs to migrate. It costs you loneliness. It costs you discomfort. It costs you disruption. It costs you confusion. It costs you uncertainty. Until you've lived it, you don't know what it costs to migrate. You don't know what it takes to shift and uproot as you navigate to plant in foreign spaces. The simple things you take for granite are suddenly no longer at your disposal. Where do I grocery shop? Who will do my hair? How will I navigate the city? When will I find friends? What doctor will I choose? Which church will I attend? When will the loneliness leave?

As an immigrant, you find yourself constantly alone in a world where everybody already knows each other. Every day you enter rooms full of unfamiliarity. Every day you travel roads full of uncertainty. Every day you step into buildings full of uneasiness. Even in my time as an immigrant I chose to be productive. I began pursuing my doctorate. I received a job counseling and teaching. I started a coaching program. I started a new business. I wrote a fifth book about starting over and here we are today. The question is what do you do with your time of migration? What do you soak up in unmarked territory that pushes your limits? You see, immigration forces you to show up as a foreigner unearthing gifts and conquering new land. Have you ever seen a foreigner go from something to nothing because they had to start over in a new country? Foreigners don't fit in, they stand out on purpose. They bestow a hunger to survive, and not only survive but win in uncharted territory. They win because their life depends on it. They win because their legacy depends on it. Migration is expensive. As an immigrant there is an understanding that the solution is bigger than the sacrifice. You don't know what I left. You don't know what I gave up. You don't know what I lost just so I could get here. Immigrants have developed an understanding that growth makes sacrificing easy. What do I mean by this? I'm not saying that it is easy to sacrifice your entire life that you've become accustomed to. What I'm saying is, when you are cognizant of the end result due to your sacrifice then it makes it all worthwhile. You begin with the end in mind. You begin this journey of newness with the end in mind of greater.

Immigrants have developed an understanding that growth makes sacrificing easy.

The Warfare of Transition

When you are migrating for better, the enemy will attack your mind. When you are migrating for better, the enemy will attack your assignment. Transition creates warfare because where you are is at war with where you want to be. It creates warfare because your reality is at war with your revelation. You desire what you are experiencing in the reality of your life to hurry up and match the revelation about your life that you had in mind. It's frustrating when you're trying to build where you are and prepare for where you are going at the same time. It's heavy when you have to mourn the ending of a season and be anxious for the birthing of a season at the same time. It's tedious when you have to supervise the departure and manage the arrival at the same time. These are all dichotomies that exist to cultivate your journey of transition. Where you are now will never look like where God needs you to be. The environment that birthed you must now release you to procreate based on the seeds that were deposited.

Immigration creates warfare because what you left places a demand on what you have to get. Who will I be here that I was not there? What have I learned from there that will help me here? Did I do enough here that will prepare me for there? The root of the warfare is the ambiguity. Not knowing what will happen next is a major factor in the mental warfare that plagues transition. The battle of certainty is a beast.

Immigration creates warfare because what you left places a demand on what you have to get.

We have this picture in our mind of what next looks like and when we're met with obstacles that challenge that, it's hard to acclimate to a new environment. Transitioning to a new season and a new territory all at once requires maturity. Every upgrade requires responsibility and when you are transitioning into greater there is a pressure to deliver at the magnitude of your assignment. It's difficult when you have to bridge where you are with where you are going because what got you here won't get you there. There is more required of you. This level requires deeper conversation. This level requires more intimate prayer time. This level requires greater discernment. This level requires stronger discipline. There is maturity in waiting.

Migration creates warfare and your destiny will always feel like immigration because your destiny will never look like your history. When you step into your destiny, you step into it as an immigrant because it's new. Can I tell you; new direction requires new directions. When you step into your destiny there should be a new identity that surfaces. Your identity has now evolved to a point where your current state can no longer house the level of purpose that has been unearthed. The most frustrating thing is when you realize the greatness within you is greater than what your environment has the capacity to handle. When you migrate, you're telling your previous season that you've outgrown it and your evolution requires more.

> Migration creates warfare and your destiny will always feel like immigration because your destiny will never look like your history.

The root of the warfare is the transcendence. When you begin to transcend from the place you are in, there is an internal war developed because your present is at war with your promise. There is a tug of war because your present can no longer hold you without hindering you. What you could so easily do, now frustrates you. Things are drying up that usually are flourishing. What comes naturally is now a fight. That season is spitting you out. It's uncomfortable to transition, but it's even more uncomfortable squeezing into spaces that no longer fit you.

The Mindset of An Immigrant

An immigrant is someone not native to a place or community. It is someone from outside of one's community. It is a person not native to or naturalized in the country or jurisdiction under consideration, an alien. An immigrant is a person who does not belong in a particular place. When someone is considered an alien, they sometimes find it imperative to assimilate and adapt to their new surroundings. When entering a new country,

17

immigrants are encouraged through social and cultural practices to adopt the values and social behaviors of the nation in order to fully reap the benefits of citizenship. Wow! Can you imagine being so new to an environment that you are considered an alien? This means you are simply in a moment where you feel you are out of this world. What a feeling, to feel like you are on the outside looking in. What a prison, to feel like you are alone in a world where everyone is on another planet.

The mindset of an immigrant is to look for opportunities everywhere. Being in new environments forces you to find new opportunities to explore, to create new memories, and engage with new people. It also forces you to acclimate to a new way of life. Where will I get my hair done? Where will I bank? Where will I grocery shop? These are all questions that are answered with new opportunities to learn about your environment. Many immigrants migrate to a new area because of the change they desire to experience. This type of reasoning can create a mindset of ambition. When you are migrating for better, this encourages a hunger to manage change before any circumstances force you to. The ability to be prepared for hardships or challenges is important. It allows you to place options in proper perspective and demand greater for your life. As the new kid you have the potency to pioneer and blaze a new trail. This unleashes a passionate sense of purpose as you walk through new open doors. It impacts your need to seize opportunities to build new relationships as a survival mechanism. As an isolated season in migration, you find yourself reinventing yourself and cultivating your growth due to the new environment you are in. As you acclimate to new environments, you all of sudden become more comfortable with experiencing discomfort.

Do you know how uncomfortable it is to have to attend every event by yourself? To walk into room after room by yourself? It's uncomfortable not knowing anyone in a room where they know everyone. Discomfort is a necessary ingredient for growth in every area of your life. Moving to a new state, I had no guarantees, just an idea of what my life would be. My identity has been forged by the purpose I have pursued while being here. There were no preconceived notions of me. I had the chance to create my own impression. The only guarantee is the approach you have to integrating into new territory. Whether it's a new country, business, habit, or relationship; starting over can be scary but it only takes you to start. You can't control the results or timeline, but you can control your focus to take advantage of being new. Being new also requires you to manage your humility. When you are in unfamiliar places, it's okay to ask for help. Quite often I'm sure you need directions, advice, or recommendations and placing your ego to the side in order to better adjust is best.

Having an immigrant mentality means having strong work ethic and being very resourceful. Possessing an understanding that no one owes you anything truly demonstrates the humility present. Inventing creative ways to solve problems when the odds may be stacked up against you is imperative as a new kid on the block. True survival kicks in and you decide that I'm going to make it. Hard work is nonnegotiable because unlike those who are right at home, you've sacrificed and given up so much to be there. There is no backup plan. I have to make this work. There is nothing to gain if I give up and everything to lose if I fail.

We all may experience small changes in our environments. While others may experience much larger changes that create the most pivotal moments of lives. As an immigrant, you experience the unfamiliar in every part of your daily existence. You are uprooted from a place of familiarity and plopped down in an unknown or unwelcoming environment. I remember when I first moved across the country. I desired to get my hair braided and did not know what would be the best salon. I literally cried in my car on the day of my hair appointment because I went through four different braiders. They all were rude and unwelcoming and cancelled the appointments at the last minute. I never thought that finding a hair stylist would be so difficult. These are definitely small things that you take for granite when you're in a familiar place. As an immigrant everything can become unfamiliar overnight and it's important to be able to harness a quiet strength.

Assimilation In The New

The idea of assimilating in a new place in order to gain understanding of its culture can sometimes be difficult. Even for immigrants who ventured here, it was said that they worked low paying jobs in order to survive in a world where they were not equal to the natives. On the contrary, immigrants during those times held jobs at the same skill level and escalated to promotions at the same rate as their peers who were from here. This gap between immigrants and natives existed due to the need for assimilation. I'm sure some immigrants arrived with a great desire to assimilate, but they just did not know how to proceed. Even their children may have attended school with children of other cultures while the parents attempted to assimilate and navigate the social norms. Today's immigrants are highly skilled and at times more skilled than their counterparts of their origin. There is quite an advantage to possessing immigrants in a foreign land. Immigrants expand culture by introducing new ideas and new customs. They introduce new expertise, customs, and cuisines to the country by expanding the existing culture. They also improve economics through hard work and entrepreneurship. By implementing research showing the positive effects of economies, immigrants increase the wages and expand the economy with starting businesses. Immigration makes the world more connected through sharing cultures and engaging in global commerce. Immigrants travel to new countries in order to seek opportunity and fulfill a dream for their family. Some also travel to new countries in order to escape a life-threatening situation.

The term assimilation helps describe the process immigrants experience being settled in a new land. A new culture and often new attitudes toward the original culture are obtained through adaptation in communication. Assimilation assumes that a culture gets to be united into one unified culture due to the adoption of culture and traits of the land. Through consistent contact and accommodation of their experiences, assimilation can truly take place. This is true adaptation. An immigrant has two types of adaptation that they experience: psychological and socio-cultural. Psychological adaptation refers to feelings and socio-cultural refers to ability. One can feel like they are a part and one can have the ability to fit the part.

Assimilation assumes that a culture gets to be united into one unified culture due to the adoption of culture and traits of the land.

Being in a new country can result in becoming more accustomed to the dominant country's aspects of characteristics. It encourages immigrants to become more aware of the social and culture practices and adopt values and social behaviors. Sometimes as an immigrant you can feel like Peter Pan always frozen in their status as the newcomer never advancing in their career, finances, or status. Immigration is a process, not a conclusion. The longer an immigrant is present, the more they assimilate and set their children up for progress for generations to come. There are also several types of assimilation that affect immigrants transitioning to a foreign land.

Cultural assimilation happens when two cultures influence each other. Customs and traditions can all be assimilated between two or more cultures. Influence may be evident between both groups in impression of each other. Cultural assimilation oftentimes occurs with regards to how people dress. When someone from a different culture ventures to a new land, they assimilate and adopt the dress code of that area. Another way that an immigrant can assimilate is through religion. Religious assimilation occurs when the belief of two groups is combined. This can often occur when a couple gets married from different religious backgrounds. Linguistic assimilation is also another type that includes two cultures influencing through speech. It can involve specifically speech patterns, accents, or even dialect. Some even speak certain languages differently due to picking up certain speech patterns from a particular area. When people move to an area where the predominant language is different from their first language, they can usually retain their original language. In addition to cultural, religious, and linguistic; physiological assimilation is also evident in immigrants. This refers to the conversion of ingested nutrients into energy that fuels the body as a greater whole. Have you ever heard of the phrase; you are what you eat? This saying is very true and refers to physiological changes that are experienced. Runners eat carbs. Wrestlers bulk up. Anorexics take laxatives. Pregnant women take prenatal vitamins. These are all examples of ingesting in order to receive a desired result. There is also statistical assimilation which refers to gathering data over time in order to obtain a clear picture of that which is being studied. Compiling statistics provides a better understanding of how things work in a new land.

Wow! Talk about assimilating! This is what involves being the new kid on the block. A new kid on the block is a newcomer to a particular place or sphere of activity, typically someone who has yet to prove themselves. Someone who is new in a place or organization and has many things to learn about it. It takes courage to be in an unfamiliar place. It takes courage to be in a new territory. When you experience the next chapter of your life, your destiny will always make you feel like the new kid on the block. When you experience new seasons of your life that require you to start completely over, your destiny will always make you feel like the new kid on the block. New job, new state, new school, new church. Any time you experience newness your destiny will feel like immigration. Have you ever been an immigrant in your destiny? Have you ever been the new kid on the block?

I have experienced being the new member at a church. I was an immigrant. I had to get acclimated to the culture of the church. I had to get adjusted to the people of the church. I had to get accustomed to the flow of the church. During my first day of membership, I was asked to preach. And guess what, all eyes were on me. They wondered who was this immigrant? They wondered who this new person was speaking over their lives? This position took transition. This position took trust in the immigration process. I thought ministry would look different. I thought preaching would feel like something else. This was so new to me, quite frankly foreign. Destiny is the only place where you can feel at home and a foreigner all at the same time. You can feel like this is where I'm meant to be and feel like I've never been here before. Your destiny feels like immigration.

You see, migration is only the ability to transition. Change is a gift. Transition is a skill. It takes skill to navigate as an immigrant. It takes power to understand that your location is irrelevant to God's choice. God can use you in this new place. In this new job. In this new program. In this new position. That's why He dried up your last season. When the famine gets bad enough people will migrate. When they get hungry enough people will migrate. When they get broken enough people will migrate. When they get desperate enough people will migrate. Make the choice today. Will you trust God in this season and migrate? Will you put aside your fears and move in uncertainty? Will you operate in courage and be the immigrant of your season?

Change is a gift. Transition is a skill.

26

The Remix-
Surrendering In
Uncertainty

The Remix- Surrendering In Uncertainty

Many of us sit and wait for a life to love. Part of the reason why we find it so difficult to love our life is because we're waiting for the hard part to be over. We must have a mindset that whatever is going to happen in our lives, it's going to make us better. Even though it may hurt, my trust is not in life, my trust is in God. If God allowed something to show up in my life, it must be here to be a teacher to me. Paul said, for I reckon that the suffering of this present time is not worthy to be compared to glory that shall be revealed in us. There are women that became who they are because the suffering taught them something. The suffering taught me to have boundaries. The suffering taught me how to grow in darkness. The suffering came in and taught me something.

There are some lessons that only suffering can teach you. These scars can work against me, or they can work for me. I have decided that my scars are seeds. The scars taught me. It wasn't the degrees. It wasn't my family. It wasn't my career. The scars taught me. The suffering made a demand on what God placed on the inside of me. There is power on the other side of suffering. There is vision on the other side of suffering. There is a breakthrough on the other side of suffering. Suffering is not the end, but if you let it, suffering can be the beginning. You will learn to love your life because God turned your suffering into good. Sometimes it's hard to love your life. It's difficult to live in such a way that you experience setbacks and disappointment.

> The suffering made a demand on what God placed on the inside of me.

There are moments where I don't care that it's going to make me better. I can't afford to not know what is going to happen. I cannot afford to walk away with another heartbreak. It's hard to love a life that you don't trust anymore. When you don't trust your life, it's hard to show up in your life the way you are meant to. It is difficult to redefine and rebuild your life at the same time. Because we don't know what it is becoming, it is difficult to love it. I don't know who I will become on the other side of this. I don't know if I'll have the same joy. I don't know if I'll have the same fight. I don't know what's on the other side of this. When you give up your comfort zone in order to be obedient, then obedience is sacrifice.

The truth is obedience is not always done with confidence. In order to be obedient, you must let go of what you thought your life was going to look like. It is better to be in the will of God instead of the will of my fears. We must obey even if it's uncomfortable. God allows you to love the people that are doing the rebuilding with you. It lets you know that you are not the only one in the rebuilding process. He didn't let you face it on your own. He showed you that you were not in this by yourself. Feeling alone is a trick of the enemy because if you ever get a revelation that you are loved and you have help, you will know that you have back up. You have help. You have weapons. You have protection. I may not know what is next but one thing I do know is that He will never leave me or forsake me. I know that weeping may endure for a night, but joy will come in the morning. I know that no weapon formed against me will prosper. You are not in the ring on your own. They may ask how can you love this life? I love this life because I know He is always with me. I love this life because I know if God is for me, He's more than the whole world against me. I love this life because I know there is something on the other side of this. I may not know what's next, but I know He's on the way.

The good is connected to the call. And if you say no to the suffering then you say no to the good and you say no to the call. You can make it through the suffering. There is good on the other side. There are so many opportunities that are making a demand on a version of you that you don't even know. There are responsibilities that are pulling on a version of you that you have to transition into. What happens if we actually give our heart to the unknown and uncertainty of what's next? We must love the uncertainty of our life. This is the one thing that can keep us from loving our life. We cannot be attached to the certainty of our life. God will not rest until He has concluded the matter that is uncertain. We must be still because God is going ahead of you. It may be uncertain, but God is clear about His plans for you. It's not the season for you to do, it's the season for you to be. The question isn't what do I do next? The question is who am I becoming next? God is going to finish it.

Sometimes when I'm starting something new, I just want to feel like I got this. When will I ever just feel like I got this? God must remind me that if I ever feel like I got this, then I will never need Him. These seasons of starting over force us to depend on God. These seasons of starting over force us to destabilize. These seasons of starting over force us to build our faith in a way like never before. This reminds me of Israel when they thought that they had it and begged God for a king. They began looking at other tribes and nations that had kings and God desired them to realize that they had the King of Kings. Upon relentless petitions, God being reckless in meeting us where we are, He gave them a king named Saul. They were immediately forced to start over and begin this new journey with a king that had absolutely no idea what he was doing. Samuel had already anointed Saul king, but he had not presented him yet. Have you ever been in a season of your life where you had to start over in a place that you were already anointed for, you just had not been presented yet? Wow! What a place to be in! Anointed but not presented! Most of us want the anointing and the presenting to happen at the same time, but isn't it just like God to anoint us, but then still keep us hidden? Sometimes people say they want the anointing, but they don't really want the anointing, they want the presentation. They don't recognize that in order to stay in the position, you will need the anointing to stay in the position that you have been presented in. This presentation requires you to start over in a way that requires surrendering in uncertainty.

Surrendering In Uncertainty

Surrendering in uncertainty in one stage of life looks different in another stage of life. If you ask someone what they would do in one situation might be different than what they would do in another. Surrendering in uncertainty is determined by the ultimate mission. As the mission changes, the surrendering may change as well. There are moments where the mission may be to get rest so when you surrender, you take a day off.

! Most of us want the anointing and the presenting to happen at the same time, but isn't it just like God to anoint us, but then still keep us hidden?

When you are experiencing depression, that same surrendering may cause you to do the complete opposite and get out of bed to get some needed sunlight. Fully surrendering to what may be easier for you is hard. We must surrender in uncertainty and take a chance on discomfort in order to find destiny. Sometimes we don't want to surrender. Even the caterpillar must surrender to the process. When it is time for the caterpillar to become a butterfly, they must be released from their cocoon. The very thing that was once protecting them in one part of the process, now has the ability to restrict them from their growth. They must surrender and move to the next phase of their life in order to fully blossom.

There are so many ways that we try to protect ourselves from experiencing uncertainty. There are so many ways that we try to prevent ourselves from experiencing the unfamiliar, but in turn we block our blessing that only growth in uncertainty can birth. That method of protection could be responsible for why you feel stagnant today. If we could have a real conversation then we would ask ourselves, can I trust the version of myself I'm trying to protect? I'm trying to protect myself from surrendering in uncertainty, but I need to surrender in order to grow. You see, not every version of you needs to be protected. If you demand every version of you to be protected from surrendering in uncertainty, then you miss God's opportunity to change that very version that requires growth. There are moments where God wants access to our way of being, but we are so committed to protecting our surrendering that we don't allow God to transform our lives. God desires to transform your life, but when you hide the areas that need the most surrendering then you disqualify yourself for the change. You're so busy trying to protect yourself from uncertainty, that you limit God's ability to shift you in uncertainty. This has an expiration date. There's going to come a time when you will have to surrender. There's going to come a time when you will have to start over. There's going to come a time when you will have to walk in uncertainty and groom your faith.

> If you demand every version of you to be protected from surrendering in uncertainty, then you miss God's opportunity to change that very version that requires growth.

Surrendering in uncertainty is not the destination, it is just the destiny. It's not your ending place, but it is the vehicle God uses to get you there. Just because you are walking in uncertainty, does not mean that you will stay in uncertainty. He is just using this season to develop your faith and unearth your gifts. This type of season requires vulnerability. When you have the maturity to recognize that this is a season that requires vulnerability, then a greater power rises up within you ready to take on the path of uncertainty ahead. It's time for me to step into something that I've never seen before. It's time for me to step into something that I've never experienced before. And I can't be comfortable and experience it at the same time. It's time for me to get uncomfortable. Discomfort will take you to places that you would never go on your own. The only way you can move forward is when you can say that I don't mind being uncomfortable. I don't mind being in discomfort. I don't mind walking in uncertainty.

True surrendering requires me to come out of the trance that makes me continue to talk myself out of what I'm called to do. I must be released from this mindset of protecting myself from experiencing uncertainty because I am truly telling God that He can't protect me. We are saying I know you called me to it, but I don't trust you to walk me through it. I don't trust you to keep me in it. When you truly surrender in uncertainty you relinquish all control. You fully surrender to God's unchanging hands knowing that He is in control. It takes true vulnerability to walk in uncertainty because you recognize that the call came with protection. We may ask ourselves what if I fail? What if they break my heart? What if it doesn't work? If God called you to it, He will protect you through it. If God assigned you to it, He has assessed you for it. You are qualified!

> It takes true vulnerability to walk in uncertainty because you recognize that the call came with protection.

Israel desired a king and God gave them Saul. They desired a master they knew instead of a Master that required the unknown. They desired to be in a position of certainty than experience a process of uncertainty. Sometimes it's easier to just know what's next than trust in God to walk you through what you don't understand. Sometimes it's easier to just see what's going to happen than to trust in God to help you get through seasons where you can't trace Him. Sometimes you will settle for a lesser master because you know it than to trust the Master in the unknown. You can be so committed to certainty that you miss when God is creating moments for surrendering. God places us in positions of uncertainty in order to show us the ability we have to be strong. We grow in power in uncertainty. We grow in anointing in uncertainty. We grow in strength in uncertainty. God knew all along that we would develop these things in the midst of uncertainty and that's why He placed us in that very position.

God will create an environment of uncertainty so that we don't rest beneath our destiny. God knows what we need and how to get it out of us. God knows what He's already placed in us and how to get us to realize it. And when we try to protect ourselves from experiencing this level of uncertainty then we prevent ourselves from maturing into exactly who we need to be. We must allow God to teach us how to unclench our ways and our plans. When we relinquish our plans, then we avail our destiny to God's divine purpose.

> Sometimes you will settle for a lesser master because you know it than to trust the Master in the unknown.

When we find ourselves attached to our own plans, then we show up entitled to the end we had in mind. But our life is not our own. God said, I know the plans that I have for you, to give you an expected end. He knows our end from our beginning. Let Him direct your path and order your steps. Let Him guide your plans and decisions. Have enough faith to walk in unfamiliarity and trust God in the process. The hardest thing you will ever have to do is let you go. The hardest thing you will ever have to do is let go of your control over your own plans. The hardest thing you will ever have to do is let go of what you had in mind. But this season we're letting go! We're moving forward! We're surrendering to God in uncertainty!

Endings Are Protection

When God is ending an era of leadership with Saul and beginning an era of leadership with David, He asks Samuel how long are you going to mourn over the loss of Saul. How long will you mourn over what I have rejected? Even though you are not over it, He's done with it. Even though you are not ready to let go, He's done with it. Even though you have not moved on, He's done with it. God is not going to resurrect something that He desires to stay buried. Some things He wants to stay in the grave. Some things He wants to never rise again in your life. In this transition, your endings are your protection. There are some things that He wants to bring to an end in your life.

When we find ourselves attached to our own plans, then we show up entitled to the end we had in mind.

Some of us are stuck mentally, physically, emotionally, and vocationally all because we will not walk in our endings. There must be an end to our need for explanations. You must stop requiring an explanation before you advance. We must shift our mindset to accept moving forward without a reason.

Our lives should be experienced forward, but oftentimes it is only understood backwards. We constantly desire to stay in the same position until we see change. There has to be an understanding that some things do not make sense until we move forward. Some things may not make sense proactively, some things make sense retrospectively. This requires us to be willing to move on in seasons where there is no explanation. Endings are not always bad, but necessary. You cannot say hello to something new unless you are willing to say goodbye to the old. The course of your life is determined by what you're willing to leave. We all have a date with God's desired destination that we can't afford to miss. He knows the plans He has for us, plans not to harm us, but to give us a hope and a future. There are some things that God intentionally does not let us know. If we are going to get to that desired destiny, we have to say goodbye to control. When we see God as a shepherd, we see Him as someone who leads our lives and guides our future. He does more than handle our mistakes, but He orders our steps.

The Allusion of Control

Giving up control is difficult, but when we think about it, it's logical. Control is an allusion. We can control how careful we are when we drive, but we can't control others. We can control putting the offer in, but we can't control if it's accepted. We can control how well we do in an interview, but we can't control if they select us. When we attempt to control our lives, then we bear the weight of what God should have. Only God can control outcomes. This is weight that we were never intended to carry. We were never intended to control outcomes. We control our decisions, God controls outcomes.

Sometimes we look at our life and ask how in the world did I end up here? No vision board could have gotten me here. No five-year plan could have gotten me here. No to do list could have gotten me here. Only God can orchestrate His plan like this. If God has something for you and me, it doesn't matter who gets there first. He will hold it in place until you get there. If you missed it, it wasn't yours. God will shift in our life in such a way that will be ahead of time. He will give us a God gap. This is when your oil and assignment don't match. This is when your practice and your potential don't match. This is when what you are doing and what you could be doing don't match. Your personal plan cannot see what God has for your life.

> God will create an environment of uncertainty so that we don't rest beneath our destiny.

Change can oftentimes appear messy, unpredictable, and uncomfortable. To get through it successfully, you must be able to persist in the face of adversity and tolerate discomfort. You must take the time to reflect and learn from your experience. All of these qualities can be housed in a term called change management. This skill cannot be mastered in a day. It takes time and experience to even understand how we process change. Some people process change differently and the effects that transpire cannot be generalized. While a one-time encounter might be the starting point, most people will require repeated practice over time to learn change management. You may understand a new skill well, but in order to execute it successfully your mind has to comprehend, perceive, and function in ways different from what you're used to. Developing capacity is a process.

That's why driver's education isn't just classroom-based. I am so ashamed of my driver's education experience. No matter how many times I prepared, I just could not pass the driver's test. I would get excited and tell my friends that I was getting my license, only to find myself disappointed in the end result. It took more than one day to build my driving skills. It took more than the classroom experience to build my driving skills. I had to develop capacity through a process. It's also why commitment and clarity are necessary, but not sufficient, for change management. You can be extremely committed to making a change and very clear about where you're headed, and still struggle to actually achieve your goals. The capacity for change management that involves habitual behavior doesn't develop overnight. It takes practice and time, especially for new behaviors to become integrated and adopted by your spirit.

Creating Capacity

When you desire to build capacity for change, a clearly defined purpose must be evident. When you are creating capacity for God, what are you doing it for? What are you asking God to make room for? Be as specific and concrete as possible. What do you need to be doing differently in order to make the change you want? When you have a clear purpose for making room, this assists in opportunities for growth. Sometimes people need help changing their behavior. Sometimes we need help shifting our perspective. This might include support groups, relationships, mentoring, or coaching. God places people in your life that you need for growth. Everything that God has for you will recognize your presence when you make room for Him. He is already placing your name in the mouths of those critical to your success. He is already placing your book on the shelves of those who are hungry for growth. He is already placing your brand on platforms that are invested in your destiny. Embrace change!

Even in transition God is still working in your life. When time meets opportunity, God will shift His plan in your favor. When the right problem comes, the Holy Spirit will bring your name and put you in position. You are not forgotten. You did not miss God. You are not a mistake. God's transition for you is divinely orchestrated. Maybe we're taking too much responsibility for our success. You don't know how I got here. God knows the best route to get us here on time. When you make the decision to make Him the Lord of your life, you have to arrest control. Even though you don't know where you're going, He knows where you're going.

Rookie of the Year

Rookie of the Year

Albert Einstein once said, "The important thing is not to stop questioning. Curiosity has its own reason for existing." This statement is definitely a true statement more so pertaining to our spiritual lives. God places our gifts in areas of inadequacy. This allows us to be destabilized and totally depend on Him because if we knew everything then we wouldn't need God. We must continue to learn and grow while being curious of new beginnings, new starts, and new perspectives. The only way to accomplish this goal is by starting over and trying something new. In order to do this it starts with reframing the perspective of the term starting over. Viewing this term as a badge of honor and act of bravery should be the ultimate representation of the act of starting over.

Oftentimes, starting over is seen as a burden or as an embarrassment that one has to start from scratch in their life. When you really think about it, those who are truly hungry for greater, maintain a mindset to continue learning. Those who desire to dive into their imagination and innovation usually possess a high degree of capacity to grow. Being a lifelong learner and having a willingness to grow requires starting over. This is actually how you would define a rookie.

God places our gifts in areas of inadequacy.

A rookie is someone that starts over in the capacity of a newcomer. They are considered the new kid on the block. A rookie is usually called the newbie due to their lack of experience in a particular area. Being a novice at a certain task or assignment is the common role of a rookie. Quite often there is a negative connotation as the underdog of being a rookie because of the inexperience at hand, but on the contrary it can be a major advantage. It's an advantage to be hungry. It's an advantage to be curious and intrigued by the unknown. You live fearlessly, uninhibited, and unlimited to the possibility of connecting your destiny to greater. When you feel as though you have already arrived, then there you lack the capacity to grow. When you deprive yourself of moving forward to the next because you fear uncertainty, you kill your capacity for expansion.

When you possess the humility to learn something new, this creates an opening to be exposed to faith changing seasons. It's an advantage to be intrigued. When you possess the humility to learn something new and lack the mindset of achieving mastery, this creates an opening to be exposed to limitations. When you feel as though you have arrived, then there is no room to grow. When anyone arrives at the thought that they know everything then they are ignorant. The blueprint of true mastery is rookie revelation. Instead of clinging to the obsession of mastery, rookie revelation requires you to continually develop a learning curve. When you walk in rookie revelation it is a choice. You are a rookie by choice and a master by practice. One way that you can gain a rookie revelation is never stop being curious. I know the saying curiosity kills the cat, but I believe curiosity secures the bag. When you are not afraid to try new things, you open yourself to new paths that you ordinarily would not be exposed to. Your curiosity will take you to places that would never go on your own. From open doors, to creativity, to transformation; curiosity will take you there. You can be curious to learn more about a particular concept or you can be curious to learn about several concepts. New insights lead to new ideas which lead to new mindsets. It all starts with curiosity.

> Instead of clinging to the obsession of mastery, rookie revelation requires you to continually develop a learning curve.

The Introduction

Despite any extent of expertise, one must avail themselves to the possibility of an introduction. Everyone should experience being introduced to something. The introduction is unavoidable. You can be introduced to a new artist. You can be introduced to a new food. You can be introduced to a new person. The introduction possesses the relentless force of the residual effects of being a rookie. When you have an understanding of your areas of growth, then this prevents the notion of complete mastery. The most bravery stems from uncertainty. It takes courage not knowing. It's okay not to take yourself too seriously. In the midst of transition, we must risk vulnerability. It takes vulnerability to admit unfamiliarity. Erasing the limitations of our own mental constructs and traditions can stifle our growth. Who said you had to do it that way? Who said you had to see it that way? Who said you had to learn it that way? Break the mold. Do it differently.

Sometimes you can be hungry for something and when God sends it, you reject it because your hunger was not enough to make you learn beyond your own traditions. Now the true art of rookie revelation is the awareness of when to use needed traditions or well implemented procedures. We are not here to reinvent the wheel. We must always remember that nothing you experience will be wasted. He's using it all. Your experience is equity!

> When you have an understanding of your areas of growth, then this prevents the notion of complete mastery.

Rookies are unencumbered by preconceived notions and are determined not to back down when faced with unfamiliarity. When someone is not moved by uncertainty about how things will work in the future then they possess the capability to develop after they have gained extensive experience. Rookies are ultimately better able to try new things and start over without the need to master it right away. They are able to explore new possibilities without the requirement of familiarity.

When you are blessed with a rookie revelation, you have the ability to ask questions without the arrogance of knowing it all. Since they have the realization that they do not have all the answers, it's more comfortable for them to inquire and actually seek the help of others. This is one advantage of being a rookie. You are able to tap into unknown resources and seek out experts who can provide the answers and advice needed. There is a sense of urgency to move quickly when God nudges them. This type of revelation allows someone to make pivotal moves based on the direction of God. Moving quickly when God speaks is a critical part of grooming our faith. God is not a God of detail, and He speaks incrementally concerning our life plan and purpose. When we are faced with steep learning curves and new territory, it's mindful to appreciate this season and maintain your hunger for greater.

Faith Over Fear

Always keep in mind, it's okay when you start over to focus on the core needs as you are hearing from God along the way. As He gives you bits and pieces of the puzzle, continue to move your feet and give God something to work with. Be relentless in pursuing your purpose even in a season of uncertainty. Their limitless spirit truly makes rookies uninhibited to conquer any dream and walk into any promise. The gift to accelerate innovation is God-given. This gift of being a rookie and pioneering through seasons of unfamiliarity pushes them to start over in the best possible way. In a new season, innovation matters, moving in the timing of God is paramount, and being available to the shifts of learning is of great value to maximizing moments of starting over.

Starting over is difficult because of fear; fear of the unknown and fear of failure. What if this does not work out? What if I'm wasting time? What if I made the wrong decision? Rookies face the obstacles of uncertainty with boldness. It's hard to start over especially when you thought you were done. The fact of the matter is, God will let you live on whatever level you settle for. His will for us is His preference for us. It is what He wants for us, but it is not what He will force us to do. When we start over, God is not a respecter of person. If He opens a door for me, He will open a door for you. He never runs out of new things. He's a God of favor, but favor is not favoritism. He is a respecter of our choices. He will respect your choice even if your choice is less than His best. Even if your choice is less than what He wants for you. You must get to a place where you are sick of settling. You must be allergic to average. Starting over will allow you the opportunity to start from scratch on a new path to receive what God wants for you. In order for you to have it, you must want it for yourself. God doesn't always give you what you want, but He will give you what to want. God places different things in our heart because He wants different things for us. If starting over is required, then that's what you must do.

> The fact of the matter is, God will let you live on whatever level you settle for. His will for us is His preference for us.

The Anointing of First

Starting over can feel unusual or even confusing. Sometimes it may not make sense. Some of us have been anointed with the anointing of first. Just because it hasn't been done, doesn't mean it can't be done. Someone has to be first. This is why you have been frustrated because you've been trying to find an example of what you should be doing next. The reason why you can't find it is because you are it. You are supposed to start this thing over because you are the blueprint. The person you are looking for is you. You had to start over because you were called to be first to do it. It starts with you! Since I can't find what I'm looking for, God is calling me to carve out a new path even if I have to start over. People will ask how did you do that? What made you start over? How did you bounce back? God leading you, is God influencing your decisions. The steps of a good man are ordered. Your steps are your choices. If you let God influence your choices, He will have your feet in rooms that your eyes have not seen. You will look at what God is using you to do and see that starting over was the key to unlocking the newness of your purpose. You thought starting over was the key to things falling apart, but it wasn't falling apart, it was all coming together. Sometimes the decisions are not obvious and take starting from scratch to truly assess all the data. God has to influence your intuition in order to create a holy hunch on that new decision. Have you ever been there? You have so many questions. Most people get revelation and try to go straight to implementation. You didn't miss God, you just missed steps. As a newcomer, you must allow God to order every step and choice. You must go from revelation to interpretation to implementation to application.

As a rookie there is a place in novelty that shows up as immaturity. There is a place in newness that appears premature. Little did you know that this season of being a rookie was a divine plan to activate your creativity and authority. God will create an environment that causes you to start over so you won't rest beneath your potential. You had to be a rookie this season. You had to start something new. You had to break into a different industry. Rookies are not a deficit, but they are divine. This spirit of pursuit develops a hunger to enlarge. This spirit of evolving develops a weight of capacity. Waiting doesn't diminish us, but it demands us to enlarge with the promises we should give birth to. Walk into this season as rookie of the year. Boss up in your newness and take the world by storm. Submit to the process even if it's unfamiliar. You were assigned to be a rookie. New looks good on you. Embrace new insight, new perception, new engagement, new triumphs.

Discomfort of Destiny

Discomfort of Destiny

Is it just me or does God have a tendency to strategically withhold information? I feel like He has certain conversations during certain junctions of my journey with Him that causes me to wonder, you couldn't have told me that before? It's as if that He intentionally omits information. It's almost like He secures my yes without completely informing me on what I'm saying yes to. I think it's probably wise because if I knew what I was saying yes to, I would have never said yes. We try to avoid adversity and don't realize that adversity is the doorway to opportunity. God is using the adversity to make us. God knows we would never begin the journey if we knew about the adversity. But the fact of the matter is, the other side of adversity far exceeds the inconvenience of adversity. You can't let a little trouble stop you from getting a big blessing. God allows us to be ignorant of what we are getting ourselves into so we can't pull out of it. We can be so anchored in adversity that we have to stay there until He pulls us out. This is the principle of perception.

Where you sit determines what you see. Because God is sitting in a different place than us, He sees things different than us. We don't realize that even though we're looking at the same thing, we don't see things the same way. God sees our trouble as tests. God sees our trials as gifts. God sees our adversity as opportunity. You can look at a thing and say, this is the worst season of my life. God can look at a thing and say, this is about to be the best season of your life. God even looked at Paul's thorn and knew what that thorn was producing in him. God saw the thorn as an opportunity for Paul to change. Paul saw the thorn as an experience of pain. They saw the same thing, but saw it in different ways. God sees things that we don't see. I'm sure Paul thought that he had never experienced that kind of pain, but God thought he had never experienced that kind of prayer.

Where you sit determines what you see.

I'm sure in certain situations you felt like you had never been so agitated in your life. And God felt like you had never been so anointed in your life. There was possibly a time where in your mind you had never struggled like that, but God saw that you had never sought Him like that. God will give you grace to endure hardship because the thing that you want Him to alter is actually altering you. Sometimes it's an advantage to be disadvantaged because you've asked God to pull you out of something, but He's left you right in the middle of it. He knows that He can bless you more keeping you there can He can pulling you out. God will let you go through the damage because you are going to experience the development.

God can undo the damage, but the devil can't undo the development. God can take away the negative impacts of the trouble, but the devil can't take away what you learned and how you grew from the trouble. There are some things that you were complaining about. You called it a break up, but now you realize that was a breakthrough. Sometimes we have a retroactive praise. We can now praise God for what we used to be made about. We can now praise God for what we used to be sad about. What we thought was rejection was actually protection. God was rescuing us from those that didn't deserve us. God was saving us from what was trying to sabotage us. God was teaching us in the midst of places that were trying to torment us. I am so glad that God did not give me what I asked for. God strategically withholds information so that I can live life knowing that there is something that I don't know.

Destination of Destiny

Even though I know everything that God has talked to me about, I need to live my life knowing that there are some things that He has not talked to me about. There is always something that we don't know. You are not always on a path to your destiny for the reason you think you are. We have an idea of what our destiny is, but we have a misconception of the vehicle God uses to get us there. We don't understand why God has us in certain places, certain seasons, certain situations. If you can handle the discomfort of destiny, you can handle the destination of destiny. It is important not to focus on the path to your purpose. God is a God that will get you to the same place as others without having to go through the process. He is the God of quantum leaps. He's a God that will put you through places that will confuse your enemies. The process that God has for you is for you. The path that God has for you is for you. It may be uncomfortable, but God knows the purpose of the path. Your attention is an investment you must make to accomplish your assignment on your set path. Your attention is expensive. You must be careful where you pay attention.

Where most people are right now is just a result of where they paid attention. Anything that you desire to accomplish in your purpose will require you to pay attention to proper things. If you spend your attention on places that will give you a return, then you won't waste your attention on things that won't give you a return. Since your mind is the place of mental real estate, don't let anyone stay on your mind that you wouldn't let stay on your couch. This purpose is personal. This season I'm staying focused on the path that God has for me. The discomfort of destiny will force you to let those go that do not have your best interest. The discomfort of destiny will force you to understand that there is a method to God's madness. What would you have missed if you had changed your route due to focusing on the way?

Are there any dreamers reading this chapter? When I say dreamer, I'm not referring to those who see with the eyes in their head, I'm referring to those who see with the eyes in their heart. The eyes in your head give you sight, but the eyes in your heart give you vision. There are some people that see your process and they see your path. They don't understand how you are maintaining such expectations through your discomfort. They're looking at your life and realize that your attitude does not match your adversity. The greatest gift that you could ever have in the midst of destiny is clarity. Clarity gives you the greatest form of compensation. This is why the enemy is after your clarity. If he can't get you to be corrupt, he desires to get you to be unclear. This is why confusion is an expression of warfare. God is not the author of confusion.

God desires us to have clarity concerning our destiny in His timing. This path to destiny is tedious, but God will multiply your clarity. Your calling requires clarity. Clarity is complicated for the gifted. The more gifted you are, the more avenues you can take. The gifted must ask what should I do? We have to ask God what route should we take? Calling requires clarity. We must be clear of this purpose and the process to get there. Some of your dreams are God's dreams. Some of the things you want, is because God has given you a desire. This destiny is personal. God has placed a desire in your heart to steward and manage. God will make you want what He wants so you can go after it and pursue it in the timing that He has ordained. We must understand the season of announcement is not the season of fulfillment. The issue is that you must have faith long enough to manage the middle season. We must get from announcement to fulfillment by how we handle the middle. We must manage the middle. When it is a God dream, He will not let you delete the desire. This is not your dream, this is God's dream. He will require you to desire it, but He won't let you have it right now. It is during these moments of discomfort that our faith is groomed. In seasons of uncertainty, learning how to walk in unfamiliarity grooms your faith.

> In seasons of uncertainty, learning how to walk in unfamiliarity grooms your faith.

The Black Sheep

No one experienced the discomfort of destiny more than David. Everything that David had gone through had prepared him for this moment. Nothing that he suffered was wasted. God was using it all. He had gone through a lot to get to where he was at that moment. He is the eighth son of Jessie. He is very much the black sheep of the family. His brothers even belittled him even when he was bringing them lunch. He had to fight lions and bears to protect sheep to get to this moment. It was through this that gave him the skill set to kill the giant. So many times we ask God to save us from something that's actually preparing us. These are the tests behind him that brought him to this point. Every one of these points were the steps of a good man that brought him to this pivot. Goliath was the usher that brought him to the palace. You cannot get to your kingdom if you don't find your Goliath. Goliath exposed him. Saul would not have given David attention, unless it was for Goliath. Goliath gave David a platform to show what his trials had taught him. He made him realize in that attack that he did not fit. These are the pivots we need in our lives to show us who we really are. These are the pivots we need in our lives to show us what direction we should really be in. The tests we experience are only the gateway to the next level of tests. Look at the preparation that this series of pivots has gone through into making David who he was. If his brothers embraced him he would have stayed. If his father had accepted him he would not have moved into Saul's house. If he had not met Goliath he would not have won a battle that changed his life forever. From that day forward he never went back home again. This was a pivotal moment. God knows exactly what to do to get you to pivot. The moment he meets Saul, he then meets Jonathon. Sometimes you experience a thing that is not the thing that you think it is. It's actually the thing that leads into the thing. Don't be so busy being mad about the thing that didn't work because the thing that didn't work, led you to the thing that did work.

> We must get from announcement to fulfillment by how we handle the middle.

Everything that you have gone through has prepared you for this pivot and for this moment. Don't despise what you have gone through. No matter how tough and no matter how difficult, it's taken you somewhere. If you can understand the very moment in your life that disappointed you, is the conveyor belt that is ushering you into your destiny, then you've got it. These light afflictions are but for a moment and are working for us a far more exceeding and eternal weight of glory. Everything I went through ushered me into everything that I'm about to do right now and it gave me the grace to pivot. Sometimes we need help in our pivoting because otherwise we would stay too long. The very thing that rejected us, is the very thing that forced us to move. Our challenges take us to places that we would not go on our own. God is using something that you don't deserve to bring you into something that you do deserve. He is preparing you and the greater the preparation, the greater the promise. You didn't even know you were that tough. You didn't even know you had that in you. You didn't even know you were that talented. You didn't even know you were that strong. It was the preparation that helped you receive the promise.

Can you imagine David just finishing a fight with Goliath, just finishing a tussle with sheep, just finishing a day of rolling in dirt and dung? Now he is being escorted into the palace. He is now walking on marble and granite. He is now introduced to the maids and butlers. He is now in an environment so unknown to him. He is now in an environment so foreign to him. God will shift your life so quickly that you won't have time to change your clothes. You won't have time to wash off the fight from your giant. You won't have time to shake off the sheep of your yesterday. In these pivots of your life where you are new, you must be able to manage the visibility. I'm sure to those on the outside looking in, David appeared out of place. You must be willing to appear out of place. It doesn't matter if you don't look like you fit in, good! I'm not supposed to fit in. I'm supposed to stand out. Because if God invited you into the room, walk in that room like you own it. It's important that in the midst of this type of transition, that you become comfortable with being uncomfortable. At this new pivot of your life, you're going to be out of place for a while. You're going to be the new kid on the block. You're going to be the one that sticks out like a sore thumb. You're going to be the light that shines in every room. Step out of your comfort zone. Navigate through the shadows. Break free from your normalcy. It's time to be comfortable with being new.

> Our challenges take us to places that we would not go on our own.

The Pivot Is Not A Punishment

The Pivot Is Not A Punishment

As you gain more life experience, interact with more people, and gain more obstacles; you have the tendency to change. Any new experiences that involve overcoming obstacles will always require you to forge new paths that are constantly being explored which in turn produces growth. The growth lies in your next move even if that means starting over. As you discover how to start over, the true key to this success is realizing how to live in fulfillment. You are definitely not the same person that you once were.

Starting over creates a time to develop new habits that push you out of your comfort zone. Actually, making a small habit change can completely change your entire life. When you decide to give yourself permission to make that change, then starting over can truly begin. You must accept the old version of you that isn't the best you which requires killing those aspects of the person that you are right now. Of course, it's natural to question starting over because your brain will tell you, "This is wrong." "This isn't you." You might even find yourself feeling guilty for releasing that side of you that you had grown accustomed to. This new version of you is what will pave the way to starting over. Don't ever allow yourself to view change as betrayal. You deserve this fresh start. You deserve the new you.

Comfortable Being Uncomfortable

Wow! What an empowering moment to have and create major moves. When you start over, you learn to accept the changes and transitions that have transpired. It's very important to understand that starting over does not mean that you have failed. On the contrary, starting over is the knowledge that there is something better out there that is uncertain. The key to that fear of starting over is the uncertainty. When you push past the need for certainty then you are able to embrace the new. Use this to propel you forward in a way you have never considered before in your life. This place of uncertainty is acknowledging who you are to the core and birthing the person you never knew you could be.

Life is about just jumping fences in order to determine your strengths and weaknesses. It's about learning to recognize and focus on what you expand and enlarge into the best version of yourself. Jump over fences this season and jump out of your comfort zone to begin a life that will fill your hunger for greater. Starting over also encourages self-awareness. As you grow in self-awareness, you begin to remove the apprehensions of moving forward to new beginnings that are unknown. This allows you to live more in tune with your purpose no matter what uncertain paths are ahead. Becoming comfortable with the unknown is important, but it's also the biggest part of fear when change is involved. Starting over is a decision that is not for the faint at heart. It really requires you to trust your instincts and truly walk by faith. Making moves on a maybe is not easy and if you decide that now is the time to start over, then it takes stepping out on a maybe. True change is evident when God's imposition fosters your transformation. True change is evident when your current state requires something greater. When you focus on something that has an expiration date, you remain stuck in patterns that consistently hold you back to fulfilling God's plan and purpose for your life. When your destiny requires a change in your life, you fall to your patterns.

> Any new experiences that involve overcoming obstacles will always require you to forge new paths that are constantly being explored which in turn produces growth.

Starting over helps open doors to a new way of thinking and fresh perspective. It can be difficult to start over and believe what may be possible for the future. When you take a leap of faith and make an effort to change, you really gain access to new creativity and vulnerability to trust the process. Starting over means having a clean slate which can be exciting, but definitely not void of challenges. When you are living in alignment with God's purpose for your life then He will prepare you for it. If God has assigned you to it, then He has assessed you for it. Beginnings and endings are a natural part of starting over. This cycle of beginnings and endings is the perfect way to promote evolution and growth while you start over. It just takes trusting God's timing and destiny for your life. It's okay to start over, as long you get to where God needs you to be.

> True change is evident when God's imposition fosters your transformation.

She Started Over

I'm even reminded of the story of Ruth and Naomi and how they started over. Here Ruth is in a new land, with a new mom, starting a new job, finding a new husband, building a new life. Can you imagine experiencing all of these transitions at one time. I can because I'm living it right now. I'm in a new state, growing new relationships, starting a new job, at a new school, in a new land. It takes courage to be the new kid on the block. Some people would rather die in a famine than pray for a rain that they can't handle. Some people would rather die in a famine than be an immigrant in a foreign land. If Ruth had not moved, David would not have been king. It takes courage to be an immigrant. It takes courage to be in a foreign land. It takes courage to be in unfamiliar territory and you don't know the rules, you don't know the regulations, you don't know the protocols. When it comes to your destiny, God will not always use what you are familiar with. Sometimes He will use the unfamiliar.

Your destiny always feels like immigration because your destiny doesn't look like your history. When you come into your destiny, you step into it as an immigrant. It's new. When God blesses you, you have to learn how to manage the blessing. Every blessing requires responsibility. And when you come into your destiny, you're an immigrant.

Wisdom In Your Wombs

The reason why God doesn't mind starting over is because He recognizes the difference between starting over and starting from scratch. Even when you're starting your life over, you don't disconnect from everything. There are some things that you need in your life that poured into you along the way. There are some things that strengthened you along the way. There is wisdom connected to those wombs. There is power connected to that pain. Someone is doing something today that is going to change the way their families do it. Someone is doing something today that is changing the way their grandkids will have to do things. If you start things differently now, then your generation to come will not have to start from scratch. If you start things that they've never seen before then this next generation will not have to start from scratch. Someone can make the decision to start this thing over to prevent the next person from having to start from scratch. I dare you to claim victory over your life. I'm starting over because I know it's bigger than me. I'm starting over because I know something new has to come. I'm starting over because my purpose is at stake. This is starting over. This is true transition. When we allow the old to break down so that the new can be built back up. God can build it back. God can give you a fresh start and when you walk into your next just know that God is always with you.

> Your destiny always feels like immigration because your destiny doesn't look like your history.

During my time of transition from marketplace to ministry, I truly struggled to trust God in the process. I thought that God shifting my business

71

was a punishment. I thought that God drying up my clientele was a punishment. In this season of my life, I quickly realized that the pivot was not a punishment. God was drying up that season in order to pivot me into ministry. This was unfamiliar territory for me and therefore I was uncomfortable because it required me to start from scratch. I was now in an arena that I was unfamiliar with. When it comes to familiarity, it's something that really grips you into a state of being that is stagnant and complacent. Familiarity will have you second guessing your purpose and challenging your future. It will have you stalling your promise and disrupting your movement forward to the next level. We are so convinced that God is using what we are familiar with, when truly God doesn't always use this avenue.

We all know the familiar story of Naomi and Ruth and how their paths were designed to intertwine. The funny thing is, Naomi and Ruth are not even of the same people. Ruth is a Gentile and is not even a part of the same ethnicity. They were not even the same age. Naomi was 80 and Ruth was 40. They had nothing in common, but Naomi's son. You see, God doesn't always use what we are familiar with, sometimes God uses what we will reject. What do you do when God puts your blessing in a house you would never go in? What do you do when God places your blessing in the hands of someone you would never live with? If He never did that, then you would never be stretched. When God gets ready to stretch you, He puts your plans in places that challenge your tradition. When God gets ready to stretch you, He puts your plans in places that challenge your comfort zone. Which lets me know that we must stop confining God's plan to a box. He desires to bless you with a plan that He's been working on before you were even born. Before David was even born God was working on a plan. He had predestined for his great great grandmother, Naomi, to go to Moab. He designed for Naomi to lose her sons and her husband so that she would leave Moab and move back to Bethlehem and Ruth would follow her.

Can I tell you that our environments are irrelevant to God's choice. In fact, God has a way of picking the most unlikely people in the most unlikely places to do the most amazing things. We often ask what is my purpose? Am I on the right track? Did I make the right choice? Sometimes purpose is set with discomfort. God will create an environment of discomfort in order to drive you into purpose. God who created comfort and who created the Comforter is also the God of discomfort. If comfort doesn't do it, God will make you uncomfortable. I would suggest to you that most of what you call the devil is just God using what you find uncomfortable to accomplish His purpose.

When you are in transition, the enemy will come with his greatest attack, familiarity. He knows that if you ever mess around and just start believing and stepping out on faith then you'll be a force to be reckoned with. This faith move is forcing you to pivot. A pivot is a transition that will bring such a fear upon you that attempts to paralyze your every move. It's a transition that will create the type of "what if's" that brings apprehension like no other. The key to achieving a pivot is to shift your "what if." Our first instinct is to say what if it doesn't work? What if there are no resources? What if I lose? What if I fail? We have to shift our "what if" and now say, what if it does work? What if God supplies my resources? What if I win? What if I succeed?

When we hear God's voice calling us to pivot, what is your response? What is your response when He needs you to push past your own normalcy and start from scratch? In our process, we cannot always control everything. While you can't control everything that happens around you or to you, you can control how you respond. God is looking for the proper response. Never allow your plans to supersede God's plans. It will never work. He took the time to create the plan, so use it!

Sometimes purpose is set with discomfort. God will create an environment of discomfort in order to drive you into purpose.

Starting over may even involve changing your environment. Our habits can often be tied to our environment. How can you change your environment without changing your location? It may just simply be changing those that you usually surround yourself with. It can also include creating a new space in your home that allows you to escape. Changing your environment could mean changing the places that you find yourself in. This can still be your start over. If you are looking for a fresh start it's a major consideration to meet new people.

Look for people who share the same goals or similar values that you embody. We are who we attract. Once you embark on a new journey, you attract those who resemble that journey. As you create new goals, these are drivers that impact how you start over. Now while there are goals in front of you, obstacles are there too. You will never be able to have a life without obstacles. They will always exist in your journey especially with a new start. The determination of starting over will lead you down a path to a better, stronger, newer you. Let me tell you, your future self will inspire those around you who didn't think you could ever start over.

Life definitely comes in seasons, changes, and transitions. And for some, these transitions can truly develop huge traumatic changes. Just think about it; divorce, moving, home ownership, starting a family, all transitions that require major change. It could also be life- changing events such as moving across the country or starting a new career that impact starting over. Whatever that change may be, it is inevitable, and it causes us to examine our values and priorities. As I experienced an engagement being called off, I began to question myself. Why did I move here? What did I want in a career? How will I recover? What should I do with my life? If you are thinking about starting over, trust me you are not alone. Believe me, it is perfectly normal to not know where you're going next. We are all on this journey of finding the best version of ourselves which sometimes takes starting over. Starting over doesn't mean that you relinquish everything that you've learned or experienced. In fact, your experiences are your best equity. Nothing you experience will be wasted.

Starting Point

Before you can make any changes in your life, you must have an understanding of where you can start from. If you are starting over, then most likely you are evolving which means your responsibility has evolved too. With every new blessing comes a new responsibility. Every upgrade requires responsibility. When you start over your work may no longer match your values. Your friends may no longer match your mindset. Your environment may no longer match your purpose. So, if your transition develops this revelation, it is important to take a step back and examine what is your value system. As you are moving forward to this new start, it is often necessary to revisit your goals. Just because it is a goal that was created in the past doesn't mean it will remain a commitment if it no longer serves your purpose. It is natural that any goal will shift or change. Let's say that you are truly ready to start over, what do you do next? It's time to put your decision into action. Make a plan. Get a coach. Find a therapist. Start the process.

Starting over is hard, but letting go is even harder. Constantly we find ourselves holding on to so many things that no longer serve us. We stay in jobs that are not progressing. We stay in relationships that are not growing. We stay in strategies that are not producing. The reason is because it is emotionally challenging to let go of something that you have put so much sweat equity in. We view the act of starting over as wasting time and fearful of the unknown. We sacrifice our purpose simply because we are afraid of starting over, not realizing that starting over is an act of creating a life that moves us forward.

Starting over has different meanings depending on how one would describe it according to their life. It could mean moving across the country or even just completely starting from scratch. It could simply be revamping and improving an aspect of your life. Whether it's a new relationship, job, or business; any change is relevant to the structure of your everyday life. Starting over can be something that you choose to or be forced to do based on your circumstances. When a person's spouse dies, they now are forced to start over as a widow. When a person loses their job, they are now forced to start over as unemployed. When a woman has a child, they now start over as a new mother. In these very moments of mandatory pivots, it may feel as though your world is falling apart. Although this is a time of hardship, it is also a moment where you get the opportunity to choose the direction your life will take.

Yielding to God's will to take this initiative, is the change you need. At the end of the day, taking initiative is taking a risk. Ultimately, it's the only way you're going to learn about yourself and your purpose. Once you start discovering your capabilities, you'll want to keep going. Once you start recognizing your potential, you'll want to keep going. Once you start perceiving your purpose, you'll want to keep going. I am a natural introvert, but once I began to perceive my purpose, I became a creative. I had to start over into a brand-new field which caused me to become an author, a preacher, and a coach. Finding my purpose launched my creative side to thrust forward. It pushed me to new areas that I had never touched. Initiative creates opportunities and allows you to fuel your passion. Always remind yourself, although you may share the road with others, no one else walks in your steps. It's up to you to recognize your gifts and walk this thing out!

Start From Scratch

God doesn't care about starting over. We care because we are thinking about the time that was wasted. But I'm so glad to know that in God, nothing you experience will be wasted. We serve a God that does not live within the realm of time. He created time Himself. Starting over does not mean anything to Him. The ultimate goal should be to get to where He has in mind and if it takes starting over to get that then that's what we need to do. When you start over there are moments where what God did is at war with what God is doing. What God did must come undone so that what He is doing can be done. God will show us how to transition. He will show us how to maneuver through the process. He will show us how to end one thing and begin another. So often we think that transition means everything is falling apart, but God sees everything coming together. The reason we don't like starting from scratch is because we don't like not knowing what's next.

Sometimes it takes being in one place, hearing what God is doing in another place, in order to move to the next place. God will never leave you in what's limiting you. You had to pivot because a new direction requires new directions. When my purpose is at stake, no one's presence is off limits. When we separate, we are so concerned with how we will be affected, but we should be concerned with how they will be affected. When you try to bring people that do not belong it affects their heart and their spirit. They are now forced to acclimate to an environment that was not even meant for them.

When you start over there are moments where what God did is at war with what God is doing.

When you hold on to your own plans, the pivot can look like a punishment. You begin to look at God and say why did I have to let them go? Why did I have to make this move? I know the pivot looks like a punishment, but you had to lose the job to start the business. I know the pivot looks like a punishment, but you had to lose the friend, to start the covenant. I know the pivot looks like a punishment, but you had to lose the apartment, to start the home owning. Some of you had no idea you would be living in the city you're in. You had no idea you would be in the career you're in. You had no idea you would be in the marriage you're in. News flash, God did! If it were left up to you, you would have never left, but God intervened and used a pivot for your protection. We've been praying that God will do it so we can go, but God is praying that we go so He can do it as we go. When you make an idol out of certainty, you limit your capacity. We want certainty before we make moves & the problem is, it takes faith. Stop trying to make moves on certainty. Sometimes you must make moves on a maybe! The steps of a good man are ordered, but the key word is steps.

Even when you start from scratch, God will continue to have expectations. Not every environment will require different expectations. God's expectation is still requiring you to participate. When we shifted into the pandemic the environment changed, but the expectation did not change. God still expected someone to be spreading the word of God. God still expected someone to be functioning in the positions He created us to. You're not going to be in a new environment without God already setting the expectation for you when you get there. Someone reading this is in a new environment and you're starting from scratch and wondering what is expected of you here. God needs you to know that He's already set it for you before you even got here. Just because it's new doesn't mean we aren't qualified for it, just step into it. It took Naomi being in one place, hearing what God was doing in another place, in order to move to the next place. She heard what the Lord was doing in Bethlehem and decided to start from scratch.

When you hold on to your own plans, the pivot can look like a punishment.

Let me tell you, God will never leave you in what's limiting you. God sent Ruth and Naomi. Orpah didn't go because she wasn't in the plan. Orpah couldn't stay because she wasn't a part of Naomi's purpose. If she had tried to hold on to Naomi, she would have caused turmoil for her life. Don't view starting over as things falling apart but view it as something new coming together. Sometimes you just have to let things

come untied. Sometimes you just have to let things
fall apart so that you have the opportunity to start
from scratch. If you don't let it come apart, then
God can't build you into who He needs you to be.
Let it fall apart so you can start over and be built
back up.

New Normal

New Normal

God is not just a God of entrances. He is also the God of exits. If we let Him lead us into green pastures, we must also be willing to let Him lead us out of pastures that we like that are no longer green. He can never lead us in if we are not willing to let Him lead us out. God desires to reframe the way we see endings and give us a new normal. Even in my life, I definitely experienced walking into a plan that I never saw falling apart. I experienced walking into a plan that I would have never created for myself.

After being in a long-distance relationship for over a year, I decided to make small steps towards transitioning my life. I picked out a ring, he sat down with my parents, he moved me to his state, planned an engagement with my friend and his sister and began planning a life together. I applied for a position at a university not even knowing that they would reach out the very next day. I received the position and had to uproot my life in three days. Who do you know that has uprooted their life in three days? I had no idea that this shift would happen so quickly. Immediately when I moved, he ended the relationship and called off the engagement. Here I am paralyzed with pain wondering what do I do next? How will I survive this? What will people say? Why was this happening? The amount of pain that I experienced I will never forget. I laid in bed for days depressed and alone. I didn't tell anyone because I was ashamed. I thought this was it, only to find that he was not ready and cowardly ended things on his terms. One thing I learned is that God will rescue you from those that don't deserve you. He saved me from a lifetime of hurt and will I forever be grateful.

> God is not just a God of entrances. He is also the God of exits.

The hardest part of starting over is, starting over when you thought you were done. When your heart is settled on what you had in mind, it's difficult to shift your expectations. When you find yourself grooming your mind to perceive a certain life, it's difficult to rearrange your affections. When your dream appears to be morphed into a nightmare, the thought of adapting to a new reality can be traumatic. In this new normal of my life, I was the new kid on the block. I had to now walk into a church and find a place to sit around people that I did not know. I had to reach out to a pastor that I had never met in my life and share my story. I had to walk into a university that I had never heard of and start a brand-new career. I had to walk into restaurants and movie theaters and malls by myself and venture out in a brand-new city alone. The anxiety that would build up knowing that I was about to enter yet another room that I was the new kid of the block in could not even be put into words. The fear that creeps up knowing that I was about to walk into yet another environment that I knew no one and I had to muster up enough courage to talk to strangers was too many to count. Again, it takes courage to be an immigrant. I didn't understand why I was there. I didn't understand why God transitioned me. I didn't understand what was next.

When you can handle the discomfort of destiny, you can handle the destination of destiny. So often, the way doesn't make sense until you get on the other side of it. What would I have missed if I had changed my route because I didn't understand the way? Too many people miss their purpose because they are looking at the path. This is not your final destination. It's not always going to be like this. This is not the place, it's just the path. Don't stop moving in the direction that God is telling you to go. Just because it doesn't look like it, doesn't mean it isn't God. He has a plan for you, just walk in it. So, what's next for you? Are you trying to place the plan in a box? Are you trying to fit the plan on your calendar? So what if it's not what you pictured or planned, it's His plan. People who plateau in their progress are people who have not mastered the art of managing new normals. One person that experienced being the new kid on the block is David. No one expected God to choose Him.

> When you can handle the discomfort of destiny, you can handle the destination of destiny.

Choosing Number Eight

1 Samuel 15:28 ESV
And Samuel said to him, "The Lord has torn the kingdom of Israel from you this day and has given it to a neighbor of yours, who is better than you. And also, the Glory of Israel will not lie or have regret, for he is not a man, that he should have regret." Then he said, "I have sinned; yet honor me now before the elders of my people and before Israel, and return with me, that I may bow before the Lord your God." So, Samuel turned back after Saul, and Saul bowed before the Lord.
Then Samuel said, "Bring here to me Agag the king of the Amalekites." And Agag came to him cheerfully. Agag said, "Surely the bitterness of death is past." And Samuel said, "As your sword has made women childless, so shall your mother be childless among women." And Samuel hacked Agag to pieces before the Lord in Gilgal.
Then Samuel went to Ramah, and Saul went up to his house in Gibeah of Saul. And Samuel did not

see Saul again until the day of his death, but Samuel grieved over Saul. And the Lord regretted that he had made Saul king over Israel.

The goal is to be sensitive in the starting over. We must sense that He is doing something. Even with David and Saul, God chose to start over. David was anointed to start over from where Saul left off. Saul was not sensitive enough to realize that he was fighting for what God did and warring for what God is doing. In this story we see what God did, being at war with what God is doing. In our lives, what we did must dissipate so that what God is doing can emerge. We must stay focused on who God is and not just what God did. He will always be doing something different. The only thing that is constantly predictable is the unpredictable. That's God.

When you limit God on what He did, then you miss God in what He is doing. When your kids begin to get older, then you have to transition what you did from what you are doing in their lives. Who God told you to be for them as a baby, is not who God told you to be for them as a young adult. You have to adapt to who you are to them now. If you are so intent on staying who you used to be, then you may lose them in the process. There must be moments where we release what God did and allow what He is doing to manifest and bring us into something new. Even if it means starting from scratch.

David knew that before He could walk into what God had for him next, that there was a sacred position that he needed to stand in for an exit from the old position. He started out as a shepherd and now he's shifting into a king. When you transition, you must discern when to undo who you used to be. There has to be a new wardrobe that you put on in the spirit. There has to be a new perception that you walk in throughout your new season. If you transition without releasing the old, then you can risk taking the old into new phases of your life. We must anchor ourselves in the middle of the transition because when God is unwinding, untying, unbraiding; what has been done, He needs nothing but the new. This is starting from scratch. Allow God to let the ground be broken up so the foundation can be set. God sees it coming together in the transition even though we see it as falling apart. God sees starting from scratch as things coming together even though we see it as falling apart.

When you limit God on what He did, then you miss God in what He is doing.

Scholars believe David spent three to six months living in the muddy, dark, lonely cave. We pick up the story there with David sitting defeated. What a low point! Most of us come to a cold, dark cave experience. We find ourselves alone, facing the shattered dreams, inexplicable pain, and desperate grief that life sometimes deals with. Cold, dark, difficult caves! David's experience in the cave teaches us about handling life at its darkest and most difficult times. And it is in this place, at this time, when he pens his prayer in Psalms 142. This psalm is a prayer. This is David pouring out his petitions to God. He cries aloud, makes supplication, pours out his complaint and declares his trouble. He describes his overwhelming circumstances, his isolation and his enemies on the lookout to trap him. David wrote several Psalms, several conversations during his months alone in the cave.

Can I tell you that God desires to revise every plan that was ever created without Him. Your plan for you will never look like God's plan for you. God's design is made up of what you need, and your design is made up of what you want. Many times, your path must pass through preparation before you make it to the promise. I would have never chosen hardship, so He volunteered me in order to prepare me. I would have never chosen wilderness, so He volunteered me in order to prepare me. Had it not been some hardship involved, I would never pivot. Had it not been some wilderness involved, I would never pivot. Our wilderness takes us to places we would have never gone on our own. The question is, do you want God's plan even if wilderness is a part of the plan?

New Caves

I know you've been crying in this new season. I know you've been crying in the new normal, but while you're crying you should be praising Him too. Because the steps of a good man are ordered by God. Even when you feel like you are in the wilderness, He still knows the end of your story. Even when your transitions have placed you last in line, He still intends to put you first. Many people start the story of David with how he was chosen and selected by God. But that's not the true beginning of the story. A lot of people don't realize that David wasn't God's first choice, Saul was. He was Robin instead of Batman. He was Scottie instead of MJ. He was Michelle instead of Beyoncé. In other words, David got an upgrade. Sometimes when we are elevated or promoted it's great to be thankful for the blessing, but maybe we should be evaluating how we were elevated. Who did I replace? The answer is, God has been trying to find somebody to do this thing right for a long time. And every time He thought he found the right person they would mishandle the mantle. So God turns to you and I believe it was missionary Beyonce that said, let me upgrade you.

When you mishandle God's promises, He does not negate His plans for your negligence. It doesn't stop being a promise because I mishandled it, somebody else just gets the upgrade. It doesn't stop being a gift because I rejected it, somebody else just gets the upgrade. And the reason why God started over with David was because of Saul's disobedience. In fact, it was so bad that God even says, I am sorry that I ever made Saul king. What happens when God regrets the day He chose you? What happens when you've disappointed God to the point where He has to find your replacement? When you mishandle God's promises, He does not negate His plans for your negligence. I want to let God know that I'm taking this thing seriously. God, you can trust me with this mantle. You can trust me with this assignment. It's some people that go hard not so you can applaud, but to prove that Jesus wasn't wrong about them.

> When you mishandle God's promises, He does not negate His plans for your negligence.

This new normal season has occurred in your life because Jesus wasn't wrong about you. I go hard the way I do because Jesus wasn't wrong about me. I rock how I rock because Jesus wasn't wrong about me. I move how I move because Jesus wasn't wrong about me. You weren't wrong to hide me. You weren't wrong to anoint me. You weren't wrong to bless me. God you can still build on me. You can build an education on me. You can build a legacy on me. You can build a business on me. You can build a ministry on me. Build on my gifts. Build on my calling. Build on my skills. I want God to sit down on what I'm trying to build. If He's not sitting on it, then I don't want to build it. Even hens sit on their eggs, and they don't get up until something happens. And when my God sits on you, He brings out gifts you didn't even know were there. Sit on me Jesus until I run out of caves. Sit on me Jesus until I get out of the wilderness. Sit on me Jesus until you crucify my flesh. Sit on me Jesus until something has to change. Sit on me Jesus until something on the inside that's working on the outside brings about a change in my life. I need every wild woman wherever you are walking into this season to cry out, sit on me.

God wants to give you the opportunity to be planted in a new season. He wants to give you the chance to develop with a fresh start. When you are hidden in a season of transition, there are things you can develop when nobody else is watching. When you are hidden in a time of starting over, there are things you can develop when you only have 100 Instagram followers. When you are hidden in a new normal, there are things you can develop when you only have the idea, but not the brand yet. Some of us are so busy trying to get to our destination that we are negating the destiny. And You can't bridge where you are with where you are supposed to be without living your destiny. Because how can we prepare to become anything if we don't even have the capacity for it? After David was anointed to be king, he went back to the wilderness. He had to continue to be hidden so he could keep getting developed. Can God call you and then send you back to your hiding place?

David was hidden in the wilderness and when it was time for him to be released, his struggles had become perfected. And God has given you this opportunity to be hidden in the wilderness so that whatever your weapon is, it can be perfected enough to stand in front of Saul and Goliath, and you can pick up a weapon that nobody has even thought about using. I'm going to use what I've been perfected with in the wilderness. And when I come out of the cave it's the same weapon, just a different platform. I've been praying in my cave, but now I have a different platform. I've been preaching in my cave, but now I have a different platform. I've been writing in my cave, but now I have a different platform. Same weapon, different platform. Same power, different platform. Some of you have been sitting on weapons because you're afraid of what Saul will think.

When God has a distinct assignment that no one understands because they're so busy looking at your process, He will have you in hiding. He will hide you for when He incubates your oil, He activates your gifts. He will hide you where there is a protector there is a pavilion. Saul rejected David because he was upset about him being the replacement. Not only did David inherit his position, but he inherited his assignment. What Saul was supposed to achieve, David had to now achieve. What Saul was supposed to kill, David had to now kill. Can I tell you, God never stops an assignment because they fail to accomplish it. There is something that God is calling you to do. Many of you may feel unqualified, but if you could just get in your mind that what you are going through is not the summation of where you are going, then you would be able to stand in the face of Saul. Here David is in the wilderness being equipped, in the wilderness being prepared. While Saul was seemingly fit for the job, David was actually being prepared for the job.

What God has for you will recognize your presence. What God has for you is already recognizing who you are. They're already discussing your name before you enter the room. They're already booking your services before you step on the platform. Everything God has for you, He's already speaking to your next and telling it to get ready for you. He's already preparing your next season and telling it to get ready for you. I came to tell somebody that feels left behind that that space couldn't be filled until you got upgraded. Some of you are being upgraded from next to priority. Some of you are being upgraded from last in line to first. I don't know whose seat you had to fill to get here, but I feel an upgrade coming. I need every insecure spirit to hear that I feel an upgrade coming. I need every disqualified spirit to hear that I feel an upgrade coming. What God has for you will recognize your presence.

> He will hide you for when He incubates your oil, He activates your gifts.

They keep ignoring you. They keep chasing you into the wilderness. They keep leaving you off the guest list. Guess what, leave me off the guest list boo boo because I'll never allow somebody to affirm me that does not know God's purpose for me. He purposely didn't allow me on the list. He purposely didn't allow me to fit me. He purposely didn't allow me to be chosen. God created an environment of rejection so I wouldn't live beneath my destiny. God created the illusion of a guest list so you would think that you actually had a say so in who had a seat at the table. Don't you worry He's already put me on the agenda. He's already placed me on the itinerary. He's already prepared a place for me. That's why David said yea though I walk through the valley of the shadow of death I will fear no evil because you are with me. Your rod and your staff comfort me. You prepare a table before me in the presence of my enemies. Endings are not evil, endings are essential. If adolescence never ends, then you never step into adulthood. If singleness never ends, then you never step into marriage. If spring never ends, then you never get to experience summer. God will orchestrate the beginning of something in order to arrange the ending of another. God is putting an end to some things in your life for your purpose of a new normal.

The New Kids

Joshua on the Block

Someone who experienced being the new kid on the block was Joshua. Joshua is a new kid experiencing a new job and moving into new territory. When Joshua is approached with this job, everything is in transition but God. He has to immediately step into this new role and not only that, but move into a new land and not only that, but move into a new way of life. They are leaving their nomadic history. They are on the brink of a new beginning. Now they must go from being slaves to being free. Now they must go from being nomadic to being owners. Now they must go from being wanderers to being possessors. They are facing a new future without their old leader.

Joshua 1:1

"Be strong and very courageous. Be careful to obey all the law my servant Moses gave you; do not turn from it to the right or to the left, that you may be successful wherever you go. Keep this Book of the Law always on your lips; meditate on it day and night, so that you may be careful to does everything written in it. Then you will be prosperous and successful. Have I not commanded you? Be strong and courageous. Do not be afraid; do not be discouraged, for the LORD your God will be with you wherever you go." So Joshua ordered the officers of the people: "Go through the camp and tell the people, 'Get your provisions ready.

Three days from now you will cross the Jordan here to go in and take possession of the land the LORD your God is giving you for your own.'

Moses was a mighty man of power and authority. Moses was in a class of distinction of his own. God said other prophets have I spoken to through dreams but of Moses will I speak face to face. Moses' rod stretched over the red sea and made the seas obey. Moses sought the face of God and prayed until manna fell from heaven. Moses declared the power of God until it was a pillar of fire by night and a cloud by day. So, when they heard Moses was dead they ripped their clothes and cried. They were almost there and now Moses is gone. The worst things can happen in life when you're almost there. They have waited for 40 years to get to this point. Who are we without Moses? How can we move forward without Moses? Life will never be the same without Moses. God let them cry for a month and then He said, now Moses is dead that's enough crying. As I was with Moses, I will be with you. I know things are tough right now, but there's been a change of plans. I know you can't see it right now, but there's been a change of plans. I know it hurts right now, but there's been a change of plans.

In the midst of Joshua waiting for this transition, he had to adapt. You must be able to adapt in the midst of transition. Adaptation is when your current functionalities evolve on purpose. When you face a challenge that forces you to develop new traits. In other words, my condition is forcing me to change on purpose. My environment is forcing me to change on purpose. My current circumstance is forcing me to change on purpose. True change is evident when God's imposition fosters your transformation. It is when God uproots every fear, every insecurity, every mechanism that we originally developed to survive. This transition is changing my survival tactics. I'm changing. I'm changing because just like Joshua I can't be a leader if I only know how to be a slave. I can't be a general if I only know how to be a follower. I can't live in the Promise Land if I only know how to live in Egypt. I can't overcome giants if I only see myself as a grasshopper. I can't lead Israel if I only know how to watch Moses' lead Israel.

The most painful transition you will ever experience is a transition to elevation when you don't see it coming. When God begins to take you higher, it requires the tenacity to survive the pressure of an elevation change. You know when you are flying and your ears pop, your stomach flips, some even get lightheaded; this is because you're experiencing an elevation change. Here Joshua is, someone who had a life of being enslaved, is now leading a nation. Someone who had a life of being a servant is now the general of

an army. He was from the weakest tribe,
Manasseh, and because of this Joshua felt
unqualified for this monumental task of taking
over for Moses. Manasseh means to forget, putting
a line between your past and your present. It's an
announcement to the enemy that that was then, and
this is now. I'm moving forward and I press
towards the mark of a higher calling, I press
towards the mark of a higher anointing, I press
towards the mark of a higher assignment.
I realize He's just taking me higher.

Adaptation is when your current functionalities
evolve on purpose. When you face a challenge
that forces you to develop new traits.

Joshua is the new leader. He has been Moses'
assistant. But now he is in charge. He didn't sign
up for this, this is something he was called
to. Called is when God brings into time what He's
already done in eternity which means the only
thing He has to call you to is an ordered step. I
don't think people understand that about a calling.
What God has for me, must recognize my
presence. And what took some people 10 years to
accomplish, God can do in one year all because He
already did it in eternity. What took Moses 40
years to do, Joshua did in 7. Joshua didn't
experience a change that God didn't allow him to
manage. Tomorrow couldn't throw anything on
Joshua that God didn't allow him to manage.

Joshua stepped from slave to general. He stepped from servant to leader. Do you know how hard it was to step in and manage all of Moses' duties? Joshua had no education, no business, no experience, no background that would prepare him for this change and transition. And whatever change and transition God has placed in your life, you have to learn to manage it. Stop crying and manage it. Stop complaining and manage it. You're not fit to be blessed if you can't manage the process. You're not fit to change positions if you can't manage the process. Joshua stepped into a leadership position just in time to cross over the Jordan. Some of the things you went through were not for you, they were for other people, so you could be in a position to help them. Some of the evil you experienced was not just so God could watch you suffer, but so God could watch you overcome in this process.

Over and over again God commands them to be strong and very courageous. As I was with Moses, so I will be with you; I will never leave you nor forsake you. And then He says be careful to obey my laws and meditate on it. And when God commands you, you have to obey. Obedience disrupts complacency when your destiny demands greater. When you have a destiny that requires something bigger than what you have, then your obedience changes your same old way of thinking.

> You're not fit to be blessed if you can't manage the process.

Your obedience tears up that comfort zone that you built. You see, a lot of people think the enemy's job is to create chaos in the middle of transition, but his job is to create comfort zones in the middle of transition. Because he knows if I ever mess around and obey God, if I ever mess around and move by faith, if I ever mess around and go after everything God has for me; I'll be a force to be reckoned with. It was their obedience that gave them access to Jordan. It was their obedience that released their promise land. Their obedience didn't negate the pain, but it negotiated the promise. Let me tell you something about obedience. I've been proposed to twice and the Lord said no, and I had to obey. I was a teacher and the Lord said there's more for you and I had to obey. I've pastored a church for four years and the Lord said move on and I had to obey.

Do you know the pain I endured, leaving three relationships that I thought was for me, leaving a career that I thought was for me, leaving a church that I thought was for me. And to cry out to the Lord, Lord what are you doing with me? And for Him to respond, don't you worry, just obey me watch me release your miracle. The safest place in the whole wide world is in the will of God. God didn't help me because I was good, God helped me because I was obedient. I'm a grown woman, with a grown God, who does grown things, and I don't have to go through you to get nothing. If God said it, then that settles it.

If you go by your plan, then you will fulfill your picture. The only problem is, God might have a different picture than you. What you have in mind may not be what He has in store. What if your plan isn't how you pictured it? What if the way He's going to work in your life isn't the way you pictured it? The problem isn't your situation, it's your picture. I know it's not what you pictured, but it's from God. I know it's not what you expected, but it's from God. I know it's not your preference, but it's from God. Are you trying to build your life by the wrong picture by what you think you're supposed to be? God is sending a picture that He has in mind for your life according to a purpose that was predestined before you were born. You have to switch the picture. When you have a picture as worthless you will build your life according to that picture. You must switch the picture. Switch the picture to what God sees. Switch the picture to what God says. It's hard to believe that it's God when it doesn't feel good. God says what's in you is from Him.

Sometimes we feel pressure about what we perceive as missing pieces. Let me tell you, there are no missing pieces. Everything in you is from Him. He made you just as He planned. He purposed you just as He planned. You have to live like the pieces in your box are meant for the picture that God has set. You're not missing anything. You have every piece that God created according to His picture. Even when I don't see it He's working. Even when I don't feel it He's working. God does not build with things that you see. When God builds something, He builds according to His picture. It's about His presence, not my picture. Did you get your picture from the world or from the word? Did you get your picture from your fear or your faith? Is your life different than what you pictured? Can I be real for a moment? Adulthood is different than what I pictured. I have struggled financially, vocationally, and emotionally on this journey of adulthood. It was not until my mid-thirties that I finally found my purpose and began honoring it. It's not what I pictured, but it's what He planned, and for that I'm grateful. God isn't building your picture; He's building His purpose.

Paul on the Block

Galatians 1:10-16
Am I now trying to win the approval of human beings, or of God? Or am I trying to please people? If I were still trying to please people, I would not be a servant of Christ. I want you to know, brothers and sisters, that the gospel I preached is not of human origin. I did not receive it from any man, nor was I taught it; rather, I received it by revelation from Jesus Christ. For you have heard of my previous way of life in Judaism, how intensely I persecuted the church of God and tried to destroy it. I was advancing in Judaism beyond many of my own age among my people and was extremely zealous for the traditions of my fathers. But when God, who set me apart from my mother's womb and called me by his grace, was pleased to reveal his Son in me so that I might preach him among the Gentiles, my immediate response was not to consult any human being.

The most important transition of the new kid on the block in human history apart from the life, death and resurrection of Jesus Christ is the conversion to Christianity of Saul to Paul. If Saul had not become Paul, we would be missing thirteen of twenty-seven books of the New Testament. He wrote 13 letters that comprise the New Testament and the most influential teachings of Jesus Christ. The irony here is that he did not walk with Jesus. He was not there for the Sermon on the Mount. He was not there when He turned water into wine. He was not there when He changed 2 fish and 5 loaves of bread. He was not there because he hated the name Jesus. The name above every name. The name that made demons tremble. The name that every knee had to bow, and every tongue had to confess. This name, He hated so much even to the point of death. So, before Saul meets Jesus, he is on his way with arrest warrants for Christians to bind them and kill them, but His sovereign grace arrested Saul right in the middle of his own plans. Jesus knew the entire time that the one who hated Him the most would be the one that would serve Him the best. This change from Saul to Paul is known as the place of transposition. The word transposition means to transfer your position, without changing your intent. There is a divine transfer that repositions you to operate in your same skills, but new posture. In Galatians, Paul said I was the best at slaying Christians in these streets, but then God set me apart. Now I'm the best at slaying demons in these streets, He shifted my position.

Saul was on his way to kill Christians, but God had a change of plans. It takes faith to become something you are not. It takes faith to become something no one thinks you should be. It takes faith to become something you were not born to be. Before Saul meets Jesus, he is on his way with arrest warrants for Christians to bind them and kill them, but God changes his plans. Jesus knew the entire time that the one who hated Him the most would be the one that would serve Him the best. This transition from Saul to Paul is faith at its finest.

Faith works best in transition when your pivot meets His plans. You can only pivot from your plans when you realize you don't own it. Don't you know we can be attached to something that God has no intention of revisiting. We can be in love with something that is unequipped for our future. What if Saul never became Paul? What if Paul didn't have enough faith to change? What if Paul couldn't pivot because of his attachment to own plans? When you're attached to your own plans, faith pivots will look like a punishment. You'll be left saying why did my job have to change? Why did my relationship have to change? Why did my location have to change? Why did my friendship have to change?

Starting over can only be effective when God's imposition fosters your transformation. God imposed on Paul's plans in order to transform him. It takes faith to start over from a murderer to a deliverer. It takes faith to start over from hate to love. It takes faith to start over from cursing the name above every name to blessing the name of Jesus. You haven't experienced starting over until you're forced to change directions. You haven't experienced starting over until you're forced to change your plans. Remember, when you are attached to your own plans then the pivot will feel like a punishment. Saul was willing to allow God to pivot his plans. As humans, we realize how necessary adaptability is. We adapt to what an environment expects from those connected to it.

> Faith works best in transition when your pivot meets His plans.

Sometimes we are so committed to our authenticity that we miss the opportunity to adapt. When we partner with God and He brings us into rooms, you have to trust that God will teach you how to adapt. You don't have to conform, but God will show you how to adapt and you will not lose the room. He will give you the right words when you need them. God needs you to bring all of yourself in the room and not shrink. As you enter those rooms God will reveal new layers of yourself, and He will show you how to walk in the room and not lose the room in the process. God will continue to navigate life with us. We must honor God and invite Him in our process.

The men traveling with Saul were speechless, but they still led him by the hand in darkness. Saul didn't understand, but he still fasted in darkness. Saul couldn't see what was next, but he still sat in darkness. Can I encourage you, that if you would just sit in the thing that made you uncomfortable. If you would just sit in the thing that made you destabilize. If you would just sit in the thing that forced you to depend on God. You would be closer than you think. Because the fact of the matter is, He predestined you to sit in things that were designed to give Him glory. I would have never chosen discomfort, so He volunteered me in order to develop me. I would have never chosen hardship, so He volunteered me in order to prepare me. I would have never chosen the dark, so He volunteered me in order to push me. Had it not been some darkness involved, Saul would have never moved. Had it not been some darkness involved, Saul would have never been Paul. Had it not been some darkness involved Saul would have never got vision. Our challenges take us to places we would have never gone on our own. The question is, do you want God's plan even if darkness is a part of the plan? Do you want God's vision even if darkness is a part of the vision? If I were you, I would just start thanking Him for the dark because sometimes we are hungry for something and when God sends it, we reject it because our hunger is not enough to make us think beyond our perception.

> Sometimes we are so committed to our authenticity that we miss the opportunity to adapt.

God is shifting your perception of this season. God wants to give you the opportunity to be planted in the dark. He wants to give us the chance to incubate in the dark. When God incubates your oil, He activates your gifts. When God hides you in darkness, He grows your anointing. How can I prepare to become something that I don't even have the capacity for? Shift your perception of this season because He's doing it in the dark. Shift your perception of this moment because He's doing it in the dark.

When God shifts your position, He makes room for your posture. Even in transition and being the new kid, He is still making room for your posture. Sometimes it's an advantage to be disadvantaged when you've asked God to pull you out of something, but He leaves you in it all because He knows He can bless you more keeping you there than He can pulling you out. He's making room for your posture. When we allow God to transpose some things in our lives, give us an experience just like Saul, we will begin to watch God reveal just how able He is. He's shifting your position even if it takes you being new.

Joseph on the Block

Even Joseph was the new kid on the block. Life couldn't throw anything on Joseph that God didn't allow him to manage. Life couldn't throw any changes that God didn't allow him to manage. Joseph stepped from obscurity into aristocracy. He stepped from malevolence to benevolence. He stepped from rags to riches. He stepped from the lowest point in his life to the highest point in his life. Do you know how hard it was to step in and manage all of Potiphar's business affairs, manage a country, manage an empire, and manage a palace? You're not fit to be blessed if you can't manage the process. You're not fit to change positions if you can't manage the process.

Joseph stepped into a prince position just in time to meditate on behalf of his family. Some of the things you went through were not for you, it was for other people, so you could be in a position to help them. Some of the evil you experienced was not just so God could watch you suffer, but so God could watch you overcome in the process. Let me tell you something, there is power in the perception of your process. There is power in knowing there's a method to His madness. It's one thing to be going through and you don't know why. It's another thing when the perception of what you're through helps you get through a little bit better.

He had to resist the urge to conform in the midst of transition. When we transition, we tend to change how we show up in the room. Joseph was transitioning when he shared his dream, but he never changed his story. God has to teach us to keep going even when people don't see it. God has to teach us to keep going even when people don't get it. God will never let you conform to a lesser form of who you are. Every time you try to shrink, God will pull you back. You can still be who God called you to be even when you face adaptability. God will help you adapt to manifestation. This moment of transition can be scary. When you get in position you don't want to mess it up and so God has to assist us to adapt. When you are just dreaming about it you don't feel the pressure. When you are just dreaming about it you don't experience the urgency. This is why God speaks to us and says I will give you the tools. I will give you the words. I will guide you in the midst of transition. I will help you to adapt to your dream.

> You can still be who God called you to be even when you face adaptability.

Joseph's anointing became even greater while in the prison. It took Joseph being rejected in the pit, Potiphar, and prison to grow in his anointing because the anointing can't be bigger than our character. We have to grow in them. God gives us things that don't fit because He desires us to grow. God develops us through inconvenience to shift His predictability. God is not according to a schedule, but He places us in unpredictable situations to make us grow. God wants to use you, but He's waiting on you to know who He is no matter what place you are in. And while Joseph is in prison, he can't forget who God is. He has to depend on the character of God. Joseph would have never been in prison if it wasn't for the lie of Potiphar's wife. This moment is working for Joseph. That lie put him in position to be chosen by pharaoh. Every season of rejection was initiated by God to bring him purpose. Somebody is in a season of rejection and every lie they meant for evil, God meant for purpose. Every trick they meant for evil, God meant for purpose. The pit was for purpose. The prison was for purpose. The lie was for purpose. So, God devises a plan so that the people who did him wrong are now in a famine. They have to now seek Joseph, the one they did wrong, and get resources from him. There were seven years of plenty and seven years of famine. And Joseph advised them to save and store. You see, Joseph understands the transition of how seeds work. He was planted in the dark in order for God to pull him out in a harvest. Joseph was planted in the dream and God pulled him out with a coat. Joseph was planted in the pit and God pulled him out with a Potiphar. Joseph was planted in the prison and God pulled him out with a pharaoh. Every dark place that Joseph was planted in, God pulled him out in a harvest. And whatever dark place that you are in, God will pull you out in a harvest. Wow! What a transition! Even when you're facing opposition, He is still walking you in favor.

It is difficult to sit still in transition of being the new kid on the block while you are threatened by opposition. Anywhere there is transition, there is distraction. The enemy will often set up distraction on the way out and on the way in transition. I wanted to write to someone that is in transition and tell you that it is the most significant place of opportunity. We often think if we can arrive there and establish something that the Lord will bless us. God does not need for your life to be at a certain point in order to bless you. I don't know if you're changing schools, jobs, locations, or friends; God is going to bless you on the way. In fact, God is most active in instability. You can believe God right in the middle of your transition and you don't have to wait until you get through it. Some of the greatest things God will do in your life will not be in your plan. Some of the greatest things God will do in your life will not be on your vision board. God will be the most active in the places of your life that seem the most uncertain.

Transition of being the new kid on the block is always an internal event. Some of us are frustrated by change because we are unwilling to endure the process of transition. If God changes your situation, but the spiritual process is not developed, then you will not have the transition you need to flourish. Sometimes when you are in transition you can feel trapped. Transition takes time, but change happens suddenly. You can experience change in your life and still have to transition to the next phase of your life. He is teaching you to stand when it's uncertain. He is teaching you to stand when it's unstable. He is teaching you to stand when it's unfamiliar even if you're the new kid on the block.

Turn the Page

119

Turn the Page

Have you ever had a great book that left you in such suspense? You wondered what would happen next, who would be involved, when the next plot would drop. Just the anticipation alone kept you on the edge of your seat grasping for air. Even the thought of an exciting twist led you on a wild goose chase of mystery eager to unravel. This next page would change the game. This next page would shift the narrative. Wow, what a place to be! This is the type of change we experience when we migrate to the next page of life. What we must realize is that change comes at a price, not a regret. We must be careful what we ask for when we pray for change.

When you transition into the next page of your life, who you are stands up in the midst of change. Who you are stands up in the midst of evolution. Your ability to hear from God is vital. Your ability to identify the unction of the Holy Spirit is vital. When you move, it takes courage. It takes courage to be in an unfamiliar place. It takes courage to be in a new territory. If you could just turn the page, you will be prepared to handle the next page. When you experience the next page, your destiny will always feel like immigration. When you come into your destiny, you step into it as an immigrant. Have you ever been an immigrant in your destiny?

Have you ever been the new kid on the block? When I uprooted my life, I experienced being the new member at a church. I was an immigrant. I had to get acclimated to the culture of church in this new state. I had to get adjusted to the people of that city. I had to get accustomed to the flow of how that city worshipped. During my first preaching experience, I was integrated into their world of ministry. I knew I was being observed. I knew I was being closely watched to ensure my delivery was aligned with their church. I was relieved when the assignment was complete. The people were receptive. The pastor was encouraging. I was no longer a foreigner. I was one of them. This next page is allowing you to walk into new territory that pushes you out of your comfort zone. This is the place where you give birth. This is the place where you pivot into purpose.

There are times where you have to follow God in uncertainty. In seasons of uncertainty, learning how to walk in unfamiliarity, grooms your faith. Even when you may not be sure of what God is doing, there should be a respect for what God is doing. You should be able to stand in uncertainty and trust Him. Don't be upset about it. God does not always give us details. He gives us just enough. Even in the days of Jesus Christ, changes brought anxiety. When Jesus was leaving the disciples and their heart was heavy, this change was difficult. Following Jesus was not easy and if you want to walk with Him, you have to walk with Him in the dark. We are just seeing glimpses of what He's going to do in our lives. We are just seeing a portion of what God can do if we would only make room.

| Success will never look like success because when you first get it, it looks foreign. |

Disruption!

When you pray for change, God answers with disruption. When God sends disruption, we cannot allow the disruption to become a distraction. Most people think that solving the disruption is the victory, but God sends disruption in order to facilitate change. You can't have change without disruption. Everything has to be disrupted in order to change. Change is disruptive. Growth is disruptive. Wherever there is change, it will always annunciate itself with the level of disruption. How you handle disruption determines how far you can go. If you can't handle disruption, then stop praying for change.

Every disruption presents an opportunity. This is what happens when your job has been disrupted, your marriage has been disrupted, your life has been disrupted. No one is exempt from disruption because it's always the gateway to opportunity. It's the gateway to a new beginning. You have to have a certain level of flexibility in order to grow in a disruption. Some people are talented, but inflexible. Some people are anointed, but inflexible. Some people are intelligent, but inflexible. You cannot grow without flexibility within the disruption. In order to survive you must be prepared to be flexible at any given moment.

You can't be more married to your plan than your purpose. Some of us love the way we praise the Lord more than the God we praise. Some of us enjoy what we do more than the God that helps us to do it. You can survive when you have the adaptability to move, change, and evolve.
We can never be defined by our location. When you are able to be nomadic, you can go where the water flows and still keep your identity. You can go where the flood is and still keep your purpose. Migration is only the ability to be flexible. It is only the ability to see that change is coming. Whenever God hits the reset button, this is a sign that God has pushed change in your plan.

When you pray for change, God answers with disruption.

Migration!

Our ability to adapt and be flexible will now become easy when we experience a hunger that changes our perception. All change has risk factors. Some people don't experience change because they are so afraid of the risk factors. They are not willing to experience change because they do not wish to experience rejection. There are some people who are more comfortable staying where they are and not evolve to the next page. There are also some people that will do whatever it takes to move to the next page. They have a mindset that they are not created to die here. They are not created to stay stagnant. When change is eminent, evolution is the vehicle.

> You can't be more married to your plan than your purpose.

Most famines are preceded by droughts. As long as there is water, there is growth. We have to be in a wet place. If we are in a place where we can have water, we can be in a place where we can grow. We must have wet environments, spouses, kids, decisions, and mindsets. There is no dry place that will be able to handle the growth that is designed to take place in our lives. The dry place is the death to your dreams. What you have planted cannot grow in a dry place and due to the drought, famines occur. When you experience a famine, it requires you to migrate. Even in migration you have an understanding that if I die at least I will die in motion. If I die while migrating at least I will die moving somewhere. It is the forward movement that gives us life. It is the forward movement that stirs our hunger. The steps of a good man are ordered but the key word is steps. You must move your feet to give God something to order. Movement is the ultimate goal of true change.

There are some people that cannot go with you even though they started with you. There are some people in your life that will kiss you goodbye even though they were connected with you. They identify themselves as not being able to take this journey with you. Sometimes their roots are in their environment more than they are in you. Their real commitment is not with you, it's with the environment that you're in. When people are not called to move with you, we must discern who is going and who is to stay. They are with you as long as you are doing what they expected you to do. They lack the capacity to be able to evolve with the migration. You would be surprised how many people who have allowed fear to paralyze their mobility.

Your fear will leave you in a level of paralysis that will stop you from moving. You talk yourself out of moving. You talk yourself out of progression. Have you ever tried to raise somebody who refused to be raised? Have you ever tried to coach somebody who refused to be coached? Have you ever tried to push somebody who refused to be pushed? They are afraid of migration. They are afraid of movement. They are afraid of change.

You cannot walk with God if you're not going to get in a flow. Our God is a moving God. He is a God of movement. Whenever you walk with God you have to be ready to move. We can't be where God used to be, we must be in the movement of God. Everything about God is moving. You cannot allow your emotions to stop your movement. Hurt if you have to hurt but keep it moving. Cry if you have to cry but keep it moving. You may be in pain but keep moving. We must learn not to make decisions out of our emotions. We must learn not to make permanent decisions off of temporary emotions. The emotion will pass, but the decision will remain. We are not rooted in our circumstances. We are rooted in our identity. If people do not have a good sense of who they are, do not create covenant with them. Movement requires the ability to adapt, and adaptation requires identity. When your identity is in check you can move in new territory and not lose yourself. You can move to a new level and still know who you are. Any type of transition or change requires identity.

Adaptation!

Transition requires adaptation. Adaptation is when you face a challenge that forces you to develop new traits in response to the imposed conditions. What do I mean by this? When you experience a situation that is unfamiliar to you, it forces you to learn how to acclimate. When you are hit with challenging circumstances, it forces you to find new ways to make it work. You find yourself developing new traits. You find yourself creating new methods. When you face something different, you respond different. Your response is a reaction to the new situation. This new condition that is imposing on your normal way of living is forcing you to change. The same mindset, insecurity, comfort zone, or process that you used before; you can no longer use to survive. You can't survive this way anymore. God is giving you new survival tactics.

When change is eminent, evolution is the vehicle.

True change is evident when God's imposition fosters your transformation. You know you have changed when your plans are shifted. Change is apparent when God's plans replace your plans. When He imposes His purpose and it makes you transform, this is change. Allow God to change you and foster your transformation. Romans 12:2 states, "And do not be conformed to this world, but be transformed by the renewing of your mind, that you may prove what is that good and acceptable and perfect will of God." He desires us to be transformed by the renewing of our mind. When our mind is renewed, our actions change. When our mind is renewed, our behavior changes. When our mind is renewed, our response changes.

Even in transition, not only do we gain adaptability, but we also gain grace. Grace is God's resources available in any chaotic event. When God gives you grace, it's because you have permission to operate in that authority for a specific purpose. God's grace grants you endless boundaries in a certain area of your life. When you receive grace, you have the capability to access resources made available to you. This is grace at its finest. When we inherit a boundary that outlines God's plan for our lives, this is grace.

Incubation!

When you transition to the next page, God takes all that you have learned while being hidden and transposes your change into true gifts. It is during this stage that your gifts are finally activated and every skill that you entered your hiding place with is now transposed into kingdom building blessings. Mature people who are evolving should be willing to serve in obscurity. This obscurity is a reminder that your new birth carries a weight that is much greater than who you were before. When God incubates our oil, He activates our gifts. You are placed in isolation for your gifts to be groomed and birthed. Incubation is the stage where the gifts are being brewed under God's glory and power. When a baby is placed in an incubator, it is used as an enclosed apparatus providing a controlled environment for the care and protection of premature or unusually small babies. They are placed in incubation in order to be provided nutrients, protection, and energy. Without this incubation they would not be able to survive or mature into the next stages of their life. While in the incubation stage, we are placed in a spiritual hibernation for the endowment of God's power and anointing. In this new environment, your condition can no longer be supported by your complacency. In this new page, your condition can no longer be supported by the same way of thinking from your past. Conditions are transformed as gifts when the perception of your affliction has shifted. This perception must be to the point where we say, this is not a condition, it's a conduit. This is not a condition, it's an interruption. This is not my condition, it's a catalyst. This is not a condition, it's a temporary glitch in His eternal grace.

God gives us the grace to handle transition to the next page. He graces us the ability to keep the faith and not give in to the enemy's tactics. The enemy's tactic is to create comfortability in transition because sometimes the hardest thing to do is walk away from what you had in mind. When you have something in mind for your life, it can be exceedingly difficult to let it go. When you are so comfortable with what you are currently doing, it can be awfully hard to give it up. God responds to faith. He is looking for your faith to move beyond your normal. He is looking for your faith to leap beyond your comfort. This is why the enemy's tactic is to attack your faith. This is why his job is to create comfortability. He knows that if you actually step out on faith, that you will be in alignment with your purpose. Purpose creates authority. When you walk in your purpose, this creates authority in that very area of your life. There is a confidence and affirmation that this is what God called me to do.

> In this new environment, your condition can no longer be supported by your complacency.

The enemy can't have authority, that belongs to God. He has all authority and power. The difference between authority and power is that power is the existence of your strength and authority is the confidence to demonstrate that strength. You can have power and not even know it. That's because you have not gained authority. Don't allow the enemy to keep you in comfort zones. You were born for greater. Take every opportunity to disrupt complacency. Take every chance you get to tear down every comfort zone.

It has been said that when people know better, they do better. I wonder if this is even true. Even in my own life I can't say that this is always true. I know that I need to exercise every day. I know what is healthy and what's not healthy. I know that I don't need the cake and the cookies. I know how to run. I know how to lift weights. It's the absence of knowledge that deters the activity. It is possible to know better and still not do better. Often, we still know better than we do. Knowing better isn't always easy. Doing better isn't always easy. We know what we should be doing, but we don't always do it. Sometimes we don't do better until we get in trouble. Sometimes we don't do better until we have competition. Whether we know better and what we do are two different things all together. We have to grow and change and make corrections. We must have the courage to change course into the next page. Sometimes it's not popular to change the course and do what is against the grain. Corrections can often have severe consequences. Getting it right can have severe consequences.

When you make a decision at one stage in your life, you get older and learn what is better so you can make the corrections. It requires humility to change to the next chapter. It requires you to go against what you said in that stage to correct where you are at this stage. You must be strong enough to stop being loyal to a mistake. Our decision to correct our mistake can create a disruption. When you see what it takes to correct it, sometimes you just don't do it. And when you don't do it, you become imprisoned with regret. You are now in a prison of your problems. You feel stuck. You go to work stuck. You go home stuck. You go to church stuck. You live stuck. Until you have the courage to stop being loyal to a mistake, you won't get the change you need. God is not investing in a bankrupt system. God is not investing in this version of you.

Determination!

There is an uncertainty in changing to the next page. Some people would stay in what they know because they're afraid of change. Have you ever looked back and rethought your choices? Have you ever looked back and wondered what you could have been if you had started earlier on the right road? You wonder what would happen if you did not become stuck. It's like the woman in the commercial saying, "help I'm falling and I can't get up." I changed churches and I can't get up. I changed jobs and I can't get up. I changed majors and I can't get up. I changed spouses and I can't get up. These are moments where you are living in regret. Is it easier to live with regret or live without it? Living without regret requires you to have the courage to change your decisions. Whatever decision you make, it will cause pain. You have to weigh the pain of not making the change with the pain of making the change. At the end of this, you have to make up in your mind that I would rather live with the pain of change than the pain of regret. I would rather live with the pain of pivot than the pain of ignoring. I would rather live with the pain of transitioning for the better than the pain of looking the other way and dealing with the complacency.

Going the way of least resistance is not the direction to go when you desire growth. Your desire should not be to be trapped in the fear of uncertainty. Yes, uncertainty does not feel good, but it's better than being stuck in a complacent place in your life. You must have adaptability and flexibility enough to change. If you choose to not make the change, you don't live your best life, you live your regretful life. Rather than move forward in change, you are stuck in what you are used to. If you are so focused on what you used to do, then you'll miss out on what you could be doing.

God wants to give you a blessing that doesn't even fit the page of life you are in. He's going to give you a blessing out of season. He's going to give you a blessing that will make you laugh. People will have their minds blown because you haven't always been a millionaire. You haven't always been successful. It's late, but it happened. It didn't come when I wanted it to. It didn't come when I thought it was coming. It didn't come when I was expecting it, but it finally came. When you have waited a long time for a blessing it will make you give God the praise. After you have suffered a while, when God comes through for you it will make you give God the praise. Waiting is not easy and it is encouraging to know that it's still going to happen. Just because it didn't happen when you planned it, doesn't mean it won't happen. You have to tell yourself it's still going to happen. You have to tell your situation it's still going to happen. You have to tell your season it's still going to happen. Get that determination that it's not too late.

Going the way of least resistance is not the direction to go when you desire growth.

Even Sarah laughed when she heard that she would be pregnant at such a late stage in her life. After she gives birth, Abraham circumcises their son while he is 8 days old. Circumcision is the cutting away as a sign of the covenant with God. The courage to change chapters is all about circumcision because circumcision hurts. Tuning the page hurts. There is no way for you to make significant change and not hurt. Not only did Abraham have to cut away some things, now he has to cast away some things. Sarah has asked him to cast away Hagar and their son. Again, change hurts. There is no way for you to make significant change and not hurt.

Sometimes change creates such disruption that you have to adjust. They are no longer the people they were before. They are now in a place where they are making corrections like casting away Hagar. This was a decision they made before things changed. This was a decision they made before they evolved. It takes courage to change because if you change, what will become of the things you have to cut and cast away? Everyone has a Hagar. Everyone has a mistake they made. Everyone has a decision that created a problem that you were bonded with. The question is, what do you do when it's time to change the chapter. What do you do when it's time to correct the mistake? Until we take responsibility for the mistakes we've made we cannot change the course. Until we take accountability for the decisions we've made we cannot make it through any transition. In order to have correction you must trust God to handle your mistakes. You can't take your mistake and your miracles and put it all in the same house. There must be a cutting and casting away. The challenge is to trust God with the collateral damage. God's grace is sufficient for your mistakes. You don't have to live in this chaos. You don't have to be stuck in this complacency. If you don't change the present, you will mess up your future. If you don't change the chapter, you will stifle your purpose. If you don't change you will miss your destiny. You need the courage to change the chapter because you cannot be the person you want to be and the person you used to be at the same time.

Let's be honest, there is collateral damage when you decide to change the page. Other people that are attached to that decision will be cut and cast away. Other environments that are attached to that decision will be cut and cast away. Other situations that are attached to that decision will be cut and cast away. Is sacrificing your destiny worth not changing? Is keeping those people in your life worth not changing? You must be willing to hurt now in order to grow later. You must be willing to endure temporary discomfort in order to honor your purpose. Obedience disrupts complacency when your destiny demands greater. Let me tell you, your destiny is demanding greater. It's greater than other people's expectations of you. It's greater than old environments that are no longer serving you. You cannot live up to other's expectations and detour your purpose. We are deciding that this season we are going into a change. We are changing to the next page of our lives for the better. We are shifting our expectations to take care of the collateral damage and usher us into the best destiny we could ever ask for. If you present your body as a living sacrifice God will do a new thing in you. Be ready for change. Be ready for next. Be ready for new.

Obedience disrupts complacency when your destiny demands greater.

The Exit Plan

139

The Exit Plan

We cannot have a conversation about starting over without having a conversation about segues. Segues are not in the way, but they are the way. Segues don't waste our time, they actually save us time. What you are able to walk into is determined by what you are willing to walk out of. You cannot say hello to something new unless you are willing to say goodbye to something old. It should be our prayer that God perfects our goodbye. If you master the art of the exit, you will never have to worry about an entrance. You cannot walk out of one door without walking into another. If we are going to accomplish God's plan for our life, we have to embrace exits.

The reason why we tend to dislike transition is because sometimes exits show up looking like shipwrecks. Sometimes transition shows up looking like a punishment. We have expectations of where we are going, but we have misconceptions about the vehicle that gets us there. It takes exits. God will transition your destination just to show you what your trust has actually been in. God never takes away something in your present that you need for your future. This exit will not be for your demise, but for a greater path to your destiny. I remember going through a major break up. I truly thought that this was someone I was supposed to be with forever. Little did I know, God had other plans. He transitioned me and took this relationship away because I did not need it for my future. I needed this exit. Sometimes we can be attached to something that God has no intention of revisiting. His plans are based on His preferences.

Segues are not in the way, but they are the way.

Entrances into new seasons are preceded by exits out of old seasons. Am I writing to anyone that feels new on you? God has a plan for you even if it's new. In the midst of exits, God's got plans for you. I know you may be confused, but He's got a plan. He didn't say you have a plan. He said I have a plan for you. You see your today and He sees our tomorrow. You see to the corner, and He sees around the corner. You see your right now and He sees your future. The exit that you're crying about now, is the very exit you will be praising about later because He has plans for you. God's plans are His preferences. God gives us His permissive or preferred will because it is what He is committed to make happen. God's preferences are not automatically our experiences. He can prefer Cannon, but we experience the wilderness. If God's preferences are going to become our experiences, it requires our participation.

Sometimes there is an obsession with entrances. We think about the doors that are getting ready to be opened. We think about the opportunities that are getting ready to come into our lives. We think about the blessings that are getting ready to shower us.

> What you are able to walk into is determined by what you are willing to walk out of.

There is also a blessing in exits. You must be able to walk into exits and perceive them as blessings too. It's not enough for God to want it for you, you've got to want it for yourself. You can't always ignore your wants. God is at work through your wants. Sometimes the things that you want to do are because He's giving you the want. He gives you the desires for your heart. Sometimes He gives you what to want. If He wants it from you, He's got to give it to you. He's got to give you what you want. Hanna wanted a baby, but God needed a prophet. So, God gave Hanna what He needed. Some of the stuff you want, God needs, so He places those wants inside of you. Everyone will not understand your wants, but it's a part of His plan.

Getting Unstuck

Because exits are a part of God's plan, the enemy desires to keep us stuck in one spot. He does not want us to exit seasons that have expired. He does not want us to leave bad relationships. He does not want us to transition out of limiting jobs. He does not want us to migrate into more thriving seasons. Satan specializes in stuck. We are not saved just to be stuck. Our seasons of suffering shifts us in a way that creates a desire for greater. Our suffering raises our standards. It is God's preference that our suffering produces hope and perseverance. His preferences require our participation. How do we participate in a way that makes our experiences match His preferences? First, we must realize that the wilderness is a stage and if we stay there too long the wilderness will become a state. It's supposed to be the path, but when I stay too long it becomes the place. We must also embrace the detour.

The way we partner with God through transition and embrace the detour is through faith. Faith is simply acting like God is telling the truth. It is a persuasion and a conviction that provokes you to a corresponding action called faith. Faith produces optimism. Faith has an author and a finisher. Optimism says it will work out. Faith says God will work it out. Optimism says it will work for my good. Faith says God will work it for my good. Faith is the withdrawal slip that we use to access what God has deposited in our spiritual account by grace. Grace deposits it, faith withdrawals it.

Transition Through Exits

You cannot get transition right if you're getting faith wrong. Transition through an exit cannot be completed without faith. Transition through an exit cannot be survived without faith. Transition through an exit cannot be executed without faith. You cannot get transition right if you're getting faith wrong. The enemy will attack you the most in the area that you need to transition in.

> First, we must realize that the wilderness is a stage and if we stay there too long the wilderness will become a state.

He does not want you to have faith in transition. He desires the detour to be an obstacle. Although all faith is significant, all faith is not the same. We must go from faith to faith and then from glory to glory. God not only wants to give us faith, but to take us from faith to faith. God desires our life to go to another level, but it requires you to go headfirst. Your mind has to move first and shift in the midst of change in order to move your life.

144

When you are experiencing change, yesterday's faith is not today's faith.

Sometimes people have faith, but the specificity of the desired plan kills it. We say, I can believe you for that, but not for that. We say, I can have faith through this, but not through this. We say I can make it through this change, but not this detour. We place restrictions and parameters on how we transition. We must refuse to be trapped by the limitation of human reasoning. When something contradicts human reasoning, we call it crazy. This contradicts reasoning because we cannot see beyond transition. Faith does not focus on what I don't have, it focuses on what I do have. The hardest thing to do in detours is believe when things are still transitioning. God wants to change what we think we have. God can use a transition to build our faith. God can use an exit to build our faith. Even in the midst of an exit, God can move in another way and that very transition will show us that God does not need one way to bless us. He can bless us any way! If it's not a door, He'll open a window. If it's not a window, He'll open a roof. If not's not a roof, He'll open the heavens. He can do it another way! Transition does not have to be negative; it can actually be a blessing.

God desires to give us divine agitation. He desires us to fall in holy discontent. We should not rest until we are resting in His will. We should not settle until it's His very purpose. This requires detours that shift our life in such a way that we become frustrated with the old and embrace the new. God is a planner. He is intentional and methodical. Whatever is a surprise to you is not a surprise to Him because God is a planner. You may be crying, but He has a plan. You may be confused, but He has a plan. You may be disappointed, but He has a plan. He may not tell you what the plan is, but He will tell you what the plan does. He said in His word, "For I know the plans I have for you, plans to give you a future and a hope." This is God executing a plan. The parting of the Red Sea was God executing a plan. Daniel coming out of the lion's den was God executing a plan. Jesus resurrecting was God executing a plan. When God makes provision according to His plan this is God's providence. God sees it before you see it. He sees it before it happens. He plans according to what He sees, not what we see. We can see today, but God can see tomorrow.

> You cannot get transition right if you're getting faith wrong.

We can see right now, but God can see what's next. Where you sit determines what you see and what you see determines what you do. What do

146

you do in the midst of a detour? We can't see what God sees because we're not sitting where God is sitting. God has plans for us. The contention is this, God is not the only one that has plans. We have plans for ourselves. We have expectations for our lives. Some of those expectations are unspoken and we never speak about it. Some of those expectations are unconscious and we never think about it. We have expectations about our career and what we felt like we should have done. We have expectations about our relationships and who we felt like we should have been with. We have expectations about our life and what we felt like we should have accomplished.

Expect the Unexpected

We have to expect the unexpected. We have to learn to manage and adjust to face something that we didn't see coming. When our plans conflict with God's plans, we have to move on from the life we thought we wanted. God's plans for us are better than the plans we have for ourselves. If we are going to move on from the life we thought we wanted, we have to be willing to move on without the closure we thought we needed. Some people are stuck after an exit because they are waiting on closure. You must be willing to move on from a detour without answers. Many of us have questions about why this happened, but we must be willing to move on without closure we thought we needed. We cannot give people the power to hold our blessing and progress up because we are waiting on their apology. No one's apology can dictate your freedom or your future. Your future is calling you and you are waiting on answers that you don't need answers for. Your future is calling you and you are waiting on an apology that you don't need validation for. Instead of focusing on what you don't know, you have to focus on what you do know. I don't know why I went through that, but I know that weeping endures for a night, but joy comes in the morning. I don't know why they left me, but I know that no weapon formed against me will be able to prosper. I don't know why I experienced that, but I do know that all things work together for the good.

This is how we pivot from what we thought we were promised. Sometimes we can be in love with something that is unequipped for our future. We can be attached to something that God had no intentions of us revisiting. We can make important decisions when we are emotionally intoxicated. We can have emotional attachments to our romanticized view of what we should be doing. When we think about what we could have, we don't think about what comes with it. When we think about having more money, we don't think about the jealousy that comes with it. When we think about having more power, we don't think about the warfare that comes with it. We have a romanticized view of what we expected our life to be.

After experiencing exits, the danger in being attached to our plans is, it impairs our judgement. This causes us to make decisions that are detrimental to our purpose. When we can admit the attachment, we can increase our discernment. When we increase our discernment we can ask the question, God is this you or is this me. When we can admit the attachment, we can be loosed from the entrapment of what we expected. We also have to acknowledge the entitlement. When you hold on to your plans, you can feel entitled to the outcome you had in mind. We feel we deserve answers. We feel we deserve our plans. We feel God owes us.

We have to be in a position where we can shift when God says shift. We have to be in a position where we can move when God says move. We have to be in a position where we pivot when God says pivot. We have to be in a position where we exit when God says exit. You can only move on from the life you thought you wanted when you realize you don't own it. It is God's plan that will prevail. It is important to refuse to revisit what you can't revise.

> When we can admit the attachment, we can increase our discernment.

Reminiscing is counterproductive. When you have gotten to the place where you have extracted all the lessons out of a situation, you must transition. The enemy will use your mistakes to keep you in a maze of misery. Once you have learned all the lessons from it, you must bury it and move forward.

> You can only move on from the life you thought you wanted when you realize you don't own it.

This past won't imprison you. This memory won't enslave you. This history won't trap you. Walk in your freedom and move forward in God's plan for your life. We must decide to not revisit what we cannot revise. Your future is better than your past. Your latter will be greater than your past. Where you are going is better than where you have been. In such a season of transition, we must trust the Savior with our satisfaction. Do you really believe that God knows what it takes to make you happy? Take the time to reflect on this question. We must trust God to make us happy. We must trust God to fulfill His plan. No matter the pivot, no matter the transition, no matter the change; trust Him to make you happy. When God says move, move. Moving with Him is better than not moving at all. We are waiting on God to go so He can help us. God is waiting on us to go so He can help us as we go.

Frustration with Exits

Some people are frustrated with life. Some people are frustrated in life. This occurs so often because we are not operating in the place we thought we should be. This occurs so often because we are not operating in a capacity that we thought we should be. Jesus didn't promise to give us frustration. People who follow Jesus will live with the joy and peace that God has for us. Although it is not God's will for us to live in a constant state of frustration, God uses frustration. Although it is not God's will for us to constantly exit, God uses exits. There are some things in our lives that would not undergo transformation had it not been for frustration. It's the frustration that gives us an indication that something needs to change.

Frustration is your friend when it comes to transition. It is an indication that we need to adjust our expectations. Frustration is a result of failed expectations. We are expecting something that we didn't find. We are desiring something that is not being delivered to us. We are not always aware of what we want until we deal with its absence. We have expectations. We have expectations about the way things would be at a certain point in our life. There are some people that didn't think they would still be single in this season of their life. There are some people that didn't think that they would be in that career in this season of their life. There are some people who didn't think they would be in this city in this season of their life. Maybe God wants to use frustration to help you adjust your expectations and help you move on from the life you expected.

> It is an indication that we need to adjust our expectations.

The only thing that is predictable is the unpredictable. We must learn to manage what we don't see coming. Something is going to happen in your life that you didn't expect. Just because you're surprised doesn't mean that you are not ready. God has been getting you ready for what you didn't see coming because He saw it before you did. If we are so attached to what we see then we will never be ready for what we didn't see coming. If we are so attached to what we see then we will never be able to move forward to what we should be seeing next. Even the people of Israel created an appetite for something that God did not have for them. We will never figure out what God has for us if we are obsessed with what God has for everybody else. We can become so obsessed with what is happening with everybody else that we create an appetite for their life and not yours. When this occurs, we can confuse greatness with popularity. In the midst of detours, what we will not learn from instruction, God will teach us from experience. When we don't listen to God, He will show us better than He can tell us. So many times, in exits what feels like restriction is protection. What seems like being left out is actually being kept for God's purpose. The immature has to stay in crisis to stay committed. The immature has to stay under pressure to pray. Many people don't know how to evolve in their reliance for God. They need an exit. Sometimes when you have to depend on God differently, you may think you don't need Him at all. When you depend on God differently, you must remember that you still need God. Maybe you don't need Him for a job, but you need Him for joy. Maybe you don't need Him for a car, but you need Him for change.

Most people don't know how to evolve in their reliance. God knows that if He elevates you then He may lose you because the only way you stay committed is in crisis. Even when you are moving on, you must remember that you always need God.

Even when you have to start over, you must remember that you always need God. Have you ever had to start over when you thought you were done? We cannot cry over what God has released. We cannot be fixated over the life we thought we were going to have.

The Exit Is Not A Punishment

When God desires us to start over it's not to punish us, it's to pivot us. It is important to stop mourning over what God has rejected. The pivot is not a punishment. The change is not a punishment. The reset is not a punishment. The exit is not a punishment. You cannot waste your oil on something that God does not want you to recreate. You cannot waste your time on something that God does not want you to revisit. God does not exist to fulfill your dreams. We exist to fulfill God's plans. God is not a God of details. We must move even without the details. Some of us refuse to move without details.

Let me tell you, God can outdo Himself in your future. God can do better for you after you move on than He can when you stay stuck in what was. Move forward and watch God move on your behalf. God is waiting on you! He is waiting on you to let go. He is waiting on you to move on. He is waiting on you to move without details. He is waiting on you to take the detour. Stop cheating yourself because you're obsessed with what you thought you planned. I don't care what your plan is for yourself. God's plan is always better than the plan you have for yourself. It's not what happens to you, it's the story you tell yourself.

> When God desires us to start over it's not to punish us, it's to pivot us.

Sometimes we have to move into the new. We have to start over. When we dictate our success on our plans that didn't happen, we are proving our disappointment in God's plan. What God has ahead of you is great. Don't allow your plan to validate your purpose. God's plan is all you need. We cannot mock God. We cannot rob ourselves of our best result.

Purpose requires all of you. One of the best ways to get over a hard past is to create an amazing future. Don't worry about what didn't happen, embrace what God is doing next! Our growth requires us to live a life from the perspective of being a lifelong learner. The day you get to the point that you think you know everything, you are ignorant. The smartest people in the world spend their lives learning. Life is full of discovery. You don't know what will happen in the next second. One phone call can change your life. Life is itself a mystery. As soon as you master it, you step into a new mystery. As soon as your kids master dressing themselves, the next thing you know is they're ready to drive. As soon as they master driving, the next thing you know they're ready to move out. Life is always a mystery. The important thing is to not to stop questioning. Curious people are always interesting people. We must never stop desiring to learn and grow in new things. We should seek not only to see what happens, but why it happened. The best question is, what did this detour come to teach me? How did what I went through serve to train me? If I don't learn what I was supposed to learn, I am destined to go through it again. We must learn why it happened in order to grow.

Experience builds equity. Everything you go through should prepare you for your next. We are so busy doing that we don't have time to think and reflect on what it came to teach me. We are so busy fighting the new season. We are so busy dodging the detour. We try so hard to fight what was, that we don't even know what is. If we would learn from it, we could gain peace from it. We have a life full of unresolved issues. It is unresolved because you have failed to use the experience to learn something that will make you better. You must extract the value out of the experience. We must understand how we can do better and educate ourselves. If you don't learn that then the person you criticize today, will be the person you become tomorrow. Not only are we learning the new things about tomorrow, but we're learning the new things from our detour that have shaped us into who we are today.

> Experience builds equity. Everything you go through should prepare you for your next.

I just want to be who He created me to be. You've been who you had to be so long that you don't even know who you're supposed to be. Instead of living in your promise land, you are living in your desert. God is calling you out of every dry place until you have a fresh start. In law there is a process called discovery. Discovery means that you collect the information and share the information. Sometimes we are in a state of discovery. We don't know who we are or where God is. We don't even realize that while you are struggling God has a strategy. Grace has serendipity. Grace will allow you to do things that you never thought you would do. It will allow you to succeed in things that you never thought you would succeed in. What you stumbled into; God already strategized. What you detoured through, God already strategized. Nothing just happens in your life. He has already determined your end from your beginning. God has already created your entire life while you are waiting to discover it. You're about to stumble into a detour that will change your life even if you have to be the new kid on the block.

About the Author

Yolanda D. Mercer of St. Louis, MO is a lover of counseling and coaching individuals to discover their hidden gifts. As a licensed educator, counselor, and life coach; it is her passion to empower others through finding their purpose. Currently pursuing her doctorate, & an instructor and counselor at Saint Louis University, Yolanda assists students in the navigation of career and life readiness. As a certified Life Coach, her mission is to help you discover your gift, define your goal, and demonstrate your growth! In this quest, Yolanda provides a coaching program to enrich others called No Caves. It is also her goal to continue to develop her own gifts as an entrepreneur and owner of a clothing boutique called Sleek Edition. One of her passions is to write books and help others write and publish books! Yolanda is the author of "Come Out of the Cave," a book designed to equip individuals to come out of their comfort zone as well as "Breaking Up With Comparison," a book designed to encourage confidence in God's plan for you. And her latest book, "Born To Be Wild," a book designed to inspire growth in transition. Through each aspect of her purpose it is Yolanda's goal to assist individuals to evolve as the best version of themselves!

New Kid On The Block

The Art of Starting Over

Made in the USA
Monee, IL
28 September 2023

43574579R00089